Pulse of the Sub-Saharan Dunes,

The Socioeconomic and Political moments: Africa in focus

MOUSSA TRAORÉ

Mwanaka Media and Publishing Pvt Ltd,
Chitungwiza Zimbabwe

*

Creativity, Wisdom and Beauty

Publisher: *Mmap*
Mwanaka Media and Publishing Pvt Ltd
24 Svosve Road, Zengeza 1
Chitungwiza Zimbabwe
mwanaka@yahoo.com
mwanaka13@gmail.com
www.africanbookscollective.com/publishers/mwanaka-media-and-publishing
https://facebook.com/MwanakaMediaAndPublishing/

Distributed in and outside N. America by African Books Collective
orders@africanbookscollective.com
www.africanbookscollective.com

ISBN: 978-1-77928-530-0
EAN: 9781779285300

© Moussa Traore 2025

DISCLAIMER
All views expressed in this publication are those of the author and do
not necessarily reflect the views of *Mmap*.

DEDICATION

This masterpiece is dedicated to Captain Ibrahim TRAORÉ, President du Faso, and all Pan-Africanists in this world and the next, and all who simply believe in repositioning Africa.

ACKNOWLEDGMENT

I am grateful to Gabriel Awuah Mainoo, the award-winning poet and the new face of African poetry for the organization, and arrangement, and to Emmanuel Kingsley Krah, one of the brilliant radical mentees.

My sincere thanks also go to Christopher A. D. Charles, the owner of Monitor Tribune, for being the brainchild of the compilation of these manuscripts, many of which featured in the journal's Africa in Focus column. I appreciate the space and the trust in entrusting me with your cherished audience.

I am forever grateful to my colleague and friend Tony Talburt, for his support. My heartfelt gratitude goes to Maxine McDonough, the editor of Monitor Tribune, for the guidance and perspectives he constantly provides.

To all my readers, I owe you gratitude for your insightful reactions and reflections that not only support my argument but also motivate me to continue writing.

FOREWORD

We live and relive history every day, and one scholar who has given meaning to this assertion is Moussa Traoré. At our first encounter at the University of Cape Coast, where I was a participant at the Authoring Slavery conference, Moussa Traoré reminded me of Africa as history in the present and the future, and as an judicious scholar of history and literature, I couldn't agree to that better. As a man with the continent at heart, he never dropped his desire to project Africa in his manuscripts, theses, and coffee break discussions anytime I visited him in his office.

He stayed true to his words. He left for Africa to help the continent, as in his words, "in any way possible," and has been teaching and writing for a wide global audience. As an avid reader, I closely follow many of his articles, which span from his literature, eco-critical, historical, law, and statistical fields. Our connection became stronger on a couple of publications I edited in which he confronts the role of Africa in World War II and the generational impact until today. Moussa Traoré's attention to detail is admirable, and his pen possesses a microscopic eye that captures often minute yet powerful details that fearlessly spark ideology, criticism, and philosophy, but are trivialized or denied by many.

In the socioeconomic and political spotlight on Sub-Saharan Africa, Moussa Traoré yearns to hold our hands and guide us through what Africa is currently facing. Not only that, in this way, he attempts to make all delve into the triggers, actors, benefactors, and the unexamined effects, as well as other possible ways humanity can assess actions and inactions, and forge resistance. In this way, Moussa Traoré's insights and motivations provoke a critique that makes his readers and all of humanity his accomplices to ideology. In a concise and eyewitness account of an insider, he brings Africa into focus with the precision of a mechatronic engineer. Although many of the illustrations are from West Africa and the Black diaspora in the Americas, the book is a Pan-African material. The author handles the data or information he is familiar with, and that comes from West Africa and th Black diaspora. The analyses in this book are focused, precise, incisive. All great pan Africanist leaders in other parts of the world have the respect and admiration of the author.

Part One discusses the socio-political landscape and turmoil of the period. With the happenings in Francophone Africa, we are given the backstory behind every gunshot, bullet, and all uncertainties behind every smoke of gunpowder, and the bloodbath of armed insurgency groups. International bodies and their goals are also captured in the light of giving Africa the best.

Part Two attempts to undercover how and why Africa's rich mineral resources impoverish her. We are open to the economic struggles of the individual who sits on these riches yet hunger and thirst for not only what they produce but also identity, currency value, knowledge, and other needs. Cost of living, utility, trade, and their impact on the economy are among the issues at the centre of this part.

Part Three, as the heading suggests, revolves around Arts, Environment, Education, and Culture. The pieces put together give you a picture of the social environment of the continent. We are presented with Africa that is rich in art forms, literature, craftsmanship, music, language, and other artifacts that attest to the continent's diversity of culture and people. Who are you: historian, literary scholar, writer, linguist, journalist, or student of life? Whatever your interest is, this masterpiece attempts to satisfy it.

— Gabriel Awuah Mainoo

Library of Africa & the African Diaspora Fellow, Aarhus Literature Center Fellow, Hong Kong Baptist University Fellow, Winner of the Samira Bawumia Literature Prize, Africa Haiku Prize, Singapore Poetry Prize, Ghana Association Writers Literary Awards; a Transatlantic Relative Residency recipient and others.

CONTENTS

PART 1: IN THE SOCIO-POLITICAL MILIEU

PART 2: THE SOCIO-ECONOMIC DOMAIN

1. The Nana Benz of Togo
2. Algeria, the legendary betrayer
3. Precious forest reserve under threat of extinction in Ghana
4. Burkina Faso and Russia cooperate in nuclear energy production
5. Fight against corruption: introduction of e-payment in road traffic violation in Burkina Faso
6. Did Africa go full circle? From the freedom fighters' conference to Antony Bliken's African tour
7. French fallacies shape considerably contemporary scholarship
8. Queen Elizabeth II and Africa
9. Post COVID Africa and Asia: the case of India and Ghana
10. Françafrique, the apparatus that sustained French imperialism in Africa
11. Ghana national security service head over ears in illegal mining
12. Africans are not insensitive to the transatlantic slave trade
13. The challenge of the international court of justice
14. New language and identity in Kumasi
15. Inexplicable episode in Burkina Faso insecurity
16. Tribulations of the African youth: Kémi Séma, the hope in the tumult

17. Cash crops hamper livelihoods in Africa: cotton in Burkina Faso and hevea in Ghana
18. Bill Gates and Africa's growing population
19. Relations between France and Africa: urgent need for paradigm change
20. Ambassador Arikana: the mouthpiece of Africa and the black diaspora in the 21st century

PART 3: ARTS, ENVIRONMENT, EDUCATION, AND CULTURE

1. The fantasy coffins of Ghana: hidden competitors in world artistry
2. Setting the record straight: World civilization started in Africa
3. First Pan-African women's conference and its relevance: Ghana 1960 remains a giant
4. Burkina Faso at loggerheads with BBC, VOA, and Human Rights Watch
5. The confusion between child labor and education in Africa
6. Precious forest reserve under threat of extinction in Ghana
7. Students' accommodation on African university campuses
8. Pan-African film festival FESPACO highlights insecurity and chronicles women's adroitness
9. Setting the record straight in West Africa: The terrorists are not jihadists, and the Fulani are not terrorists
10. George Padmore: A Caribbean key artisan of Africa's decolonization
11. Greetings in Africa

2. Music and dance in Burkina Faso: A look across the spectrum
3. Hip hop, national, and Pan African identity in Burkina Faso
4. The map of the world is about to change: Africa is splitting into two
5. Strike fever in Ghanaian universities
6. The truth behind school textbooks in French-speaking Africa: Western-driven content and market
7. Algeria, the legendary betrayer
8. Skin bleaching: a practice losing ground in Africa
9. France vents her anger on black journalists
10. Trauma of children in Burkina Faso: a sequel of the war on terror
11. Bill Gates and Africa's growing population
12. The fantasy coffins of Ghana: hidden competitors in world artistry
13. Pan-African film festival FESPACO highlights insecurity and chronicles women's adroitness
14. First black man to win the most prestigious prize in architecture

IN AN AFRICAN'S DREAM
UNKNOWN VOICES IN VOICES

— Gabriel Awuah Mainoo
(from Travellers Gather Dust and Lust)

There is a wall parting us
You're made of stars and fire//
beauty & repulsion//
than a good name//
the irony survive//
knows us better//
you kill a man//
in the rising incense//
the blood revives//
on G/god (s)//
this cathedral…

color?
let's call the difference
In Africa riches are better
Only those who know
Often the problem
On this land, you kill a problem,
So we finish the business
It doesn't end there
D o g (s); dependent
This is how we live in

PART I

IN THE SOCIO-POLITICAL MILIEU

AFRICA IN TODAY'S WORLD: FROM BIPOLARITY TO MULTIPOLARITY

The world has been qualified in various ways, and each time, power or salient features like economic and military power were the means that enabled the formation of a pole or a polarity. It therefore becomes easy to understand why the main term used in geopolitics after World War 2 was "bipolarity" or a world that could best be described as a juxtaposition or a [careful] cohabitation of 2 poles: the Eastern Bloc and the Western one, the capitalist pole and the communist one and the former referred to the Soviet Union and her allies and the latter was the appellation of the free-market US and her allies. The allies of each polarity were scattered all across the world, on almost every continent. Along the line, that context of multi-polarity saw the emergence of the Non-Aligned Movement (NAM) in 1961, another third category that claimed to associate with neither the Eastern nor Western bloc, and some of those countries were Ghana, Cuba, Egypt, India, Indonesia, Yugoslavia, etc. The group aimed at protecting the interests of newly independent countries in the context of the Cold War (between the Soviet Union and the USA), and it also intended to counterbalance the rapid bipolarization of the world. After the United Nations, the Non-Aligned Movement was the largest grouping of states in the world. Some of the characteristics of the non-aligned group were nationalism, independence, and anti-imperialism. There was much criticism leveled against them, regarding their genuineness; some critics refuted their "non-aligned" nature and claimed that those countries had secret ties with the Eastern bloc or the Western one. The truth is that the non-aligned camp or group did not last so long;

it began to dismantle after the end of the Cold War and when the African "independent" countries started experiencing the first coups d'état. The new African regimes espoused the capitalist or Western path, the communist way, or the Eastern one. Most of those countries became capitalist, though, since the coups were orchestrated by European capitalist powers and the US.

The dismantling of the USSR around the 1990s, with Gorbachev as president in the Soviet Union and Reagan as president in the US, led to a unipolar world, led by the USA that suddenly became the sole superpower in the world. Many countries were opposed to American hegemony, but they never succeeded in forming a bloc that could stand up to the US. Two other important components are being added to the analysis, or attempt to "classify" the world today: the Chinese factor and the new military and anti-French stance in West Africa. It will certainly be useful to look at the way those 2 new elements impact the global scene. The term 'bipolarity' is being replaced with 'multi-polarity' now, since several dynamics impose themselves on the map of the world. The geopolitical trajectory, therefore, can be simplified as follows, to some extent. (I am hedging here because someone could think that a polarity or other polarities existed before World War II. That could lead us into a more profound and lengthier debate that would need historical and anthropological data and analyses). So, we could say that the general course of the geopolitical journey of the world has been: the bipolarity of post-World War II, the unipolarity engendered by the dislocation of the Communist bloc and the USSR, the non-aligned camp that emerged and lived in *"progressivist"* developing countries mostly in Africa, Asia, and the Americas.

The ensuing multipolarity came to be dominated by the sudden emergence of Chinese power on the world political scene and the global market. After the Tiananmen Square Massacre of 1989, in 1992 precisely, reforms were adopted and the hardline communist policy of China was replaced by a call for more openness, liberalism, and freedom of speech; all those changes were demanded by a younger and new generation of students and also scholars who were products of Western universities. The US, through the CIA, Hong Kong, and several other liberal market-driven countries, then slipped into Chinese politics, and as a result, China is today practicing what is generally called a "hybrid communism", or a form of communism with capitalist traits. That complex feature somehow explains why China is now playing such a vital role in the world market, to such an extent that all nations in the world respect the economic and military weight of that country. Data from the World Bank shows that China experienced years of high GDP growth and its economy ballooned more than tenfold between the turn of the century and 2021, from $1.2 trillion to nearly $18 trillion. By contrast, the GDP of the United States, the world's largest economy, is a little more than double its size in 2000. China is therefore the world's biggest economy in the world, after the US. China also has one of the fastest-growing economies in the world, according to a 2023 survey, while the US is not on the list. China is therefore recovering from the impact of the COVID-19 pandemic. The politico-cultural strategy of the Confucius Institutes that are being implanted in almost every country on earth contributes to safeguarding the Chinese influence in the world. China is therefore perceived by many as the new colonizer in the world.

The BRICS (Brazil, Russia, India, China and South Africa) is the acronym for the major emerging economies (initially BRIC founded in 2001, before South Africa was added in 2009) is the notion that captures to a great extend the current state of multi-polarities and the most recent development in the discussion on multi-polarities is the current sociopolitical manifestations occurring in Africa, especially in West Africa where the ground is fertile for military coups occasioned by jihadist attacks in most cases and their corollaries, and anti-imperialist approaches, especially the rejection of French neocolonialism. Certain sources claim that France produces the jihadists who are often members of the French Foreign Legion in most cases, and ironically, the strikes of those jihadists lead to the national revolts against France, as we notice in the recent military takeovers in West Africa. The obvious new factor is the embrace of Russian power, presence, and assistance in all those countries where France is being booted out. Several factors account for this new phenomenon: the much-talked-about efficiency of the Russian Wagner mercenary group in the combat against the jihadists, the historical fact that Russia did not colonize any African country, and lastly, the fact that many of the military officers leading those coups were trained in Russia. All the African nations that are severing ties with France are soliciting strong alliances with Russia. One would therefore not be wrong in saying that the 'Russia' component of BRICS is (at least, so far) replacing France in terms of political and economic influence in West Africa.

There is therefore no moment when the term 'multi-polarities' has been more relevant than now.

TRAUMA OF CHILDREN IN BURKINA FASO: A SEQUEL OF THE WAR ON TERROR

The war against terror in Burkina is proving to be long, with each camp becoming tougher and tougher. The war which started a decade ago has particularities: the main cause behind it has not been clearly determined, only speculations abound. Another special feature of the conflict lies, as the military chiefs of the country and the president asserted on several occasions, is the fact that it is a war against an unidentified enemy. All that is known is that the opposing camp is made of terrorists, aligned to larger terrorist groups like the Islamic State and Al-Qaeda. Other speculations attribute an Islamic feature to it, and that factor was quickly eliminated by religious groups, especially Islamic scholars who stressed the difference between jihad and terrorism. As a result, the Burkinabè media does not refer to the enemy camp as jihadists. Aside from such a multifacetedness, the long conflict is having scary and devastating effects on adults and children.

Adults are certainly victims of this conflict and the "victory" of the terrorists generated regime changes. That victory was measured by the new territories that the enemy conquered. Civilian regimes got toppled by the military and the army itself showed some dissension. The first putsch ended up with Lieutenant Colonel Paul Henri Damiba as head of state but his failure to strengthen the national army and administer heavy blows to the terrorists, as the population demanded ultimately brought about the end of his regime. Certain analysts contend that each of these two coups was carried out by the same group of young army officers who disapproved of the laissez-faire attitude of the civilian president Roch Marc Christian Kaboré. So the "irresponsibility" of Lieutenant Colonel Damiba paved the way for the second coup that brought Captain Traoré to power. The general population approves of his governance. Sustainable development based on self -sufficiency, patriotism and anti-neocolonialism is the corner stone of his agenda. Terrorists who were conquering vaster and vaster territories are now being dealt heavy blows with new equipment purchased from Russia most of the time, and the military co-operation between Russia and Turkey is helping.

The Russia-Burkina cooperation has reached such a level that the presence of Russian soldiers is no more a secret in the country of the incorruptible Man. Recent news circulated pictures of Russian military personnel among the security of President Traoré. Citizens are in support of the war against terrorists. Almost every item purchased carries a tax which is channeled towards the support of the national troops and in certain cases, individuals disburse huge amounts of money as their contribution to the support of the national troops. So, the general tableau is that the largest part of the Burkinabè are in favour of the current regime in Ouagadougou. I often hear during discussions with friends and acquaintances that some people are not in favour of the regime's policy because its priority is the army and the anti-terror war and nothing else. Such arguments are defeated when we think that re-conquering the national territory and putting an end to a war which is lasting so long are the sine qua non for any development plan. The second most preponderant criticism against the MPSR2 Regime (which was ultimately given a 5 year transitional mandate) is that human rights are violated and dissenting voices are muffled by the habit of sending such critics to the anti-terror battle field. Reliable sources have it that such critics of the military regime are not put at the forefront on the battle field. They are made to face situations like "comforting a soldier whose limps were amputated due to injuries, or consoling a widow and orphans left behind by a soldier of the national army who lost his life on the battle field". I was told that such an assignment makes those opponents to the regime in power to have a feel of the reality on the terrain and when they return after such an experience, most of them show their support for the government and others choose to remain silent and voice out no condemnation of the war-centered governance of the transitional government.

An aspect that has been of much concern to me is the psychological and psychic consequence of this conflict on civilians and combatants. Several considerations are made in favor of the victims and the volunteer forces. Employment is made easier for some of them; those who were unemployed get regular jobs most of time in the military or paramilitary forces or services. The children of fallen soldiers are given opportunities to smoothen their education. But there is a more vital aspect that deserves attention: the trauma visited on the relatives of the victims of the war on terror. Weeks ago, a PhD dissertation was defended at the Joseph Ki-Zerbo University, Ouagadougou on the psychological effect of the war on the police personnel. The thesis was highly rated, well appreciated and more research of that type was encouraged. Many psychologists and psychiatrists in Burkina today are overburdened because of the heavy workload they handle. Some of them are brilliant Psychology postgraduate students who work with NGOs in order to treat or alleviate the trauma of people who have witnessed the following, among others: a group of terrorists round up civilians and shoot or behead the husband(s), fathers(s) in presence of their family members. In certain cases, the cruelty is heightened, children see their father being slaughtered. Efforts must now consider the traumatic burden of this war on the Burkinabè populations. One must commend the media for running headlines like the following: "In Burkina Faso, a growing number of children are traumatized by war"(*Africanews*, June 6-7 2024).

The guilt of survival is the tactic used by the gunmen who enter villages in this conflict. They generally execute the men and other relatives under the eyes of mothers and their children. Two (2) million people are displaced in the country and 60% of those displaced people are children. The trauma aspect is becoming more and more acute since mental health is limited, as in most sub-Saharan countries and in such a context, mental treatment is reserved to the most severe cases. With a population of 20 million, Burkina has 113 mental health professionals including 11 psychiatrists. The general attitude is also the conviction that "children have not seen anything, nothing therefore happened to them, it is fine", an attitude that a Red Cross health coordinator in Burkina laments. The treatment of trauma in children relies heavily on women, mothers who can detect signs of trauma in 3-4 year old children and close monitoring reveals that effective treatment is more likely to be achieved when children have a parental figure in their lives. Mass killings are common in the northern region of the country which experiences most of the clashes because of its strategic location. 20,000 civilians have allegedly been killed by volunteer national forces who suspect the civilians of cooperating with the enemy camp, the terrorists. The general scenario is that after the attacks, fearing other attacks, mothers walk long distances with their children and other children, with no money, and relocate among relatively safe communities. This is precisely when they start detecting signs of Post-Traumatic Stress Disorder (PTSD) in the children: they have nightmares and cannot sleep at night. During the day they do not play with other children. In such cases, mothers are connected to appropriate health workers who use the practice of home visits and art. They encourage children to draw their fears and talk about them.

Traditional medicine practitioners claim that they also play an important role in this situation. One of them is reported to have said that he cures about 5 children every month. These "healers" adjust their treatment to the trauma suffered. The attacks of health facilities have caused their closure and that compounds the problem since 3.6 million people are left with no access to basic health care and mental health is obviously non-existent.

These millions of displaced mothers and children rely on limited mental health treatment but we need to recognize that the few mental health workers on the terrain are doing their best. The low ratio patient to mental health specialist is the main problem. Another solace is found in the host communities. The majority of mothers (who themselves are traumatized in most cases) and their traumatized children find those host communities to be welcoming, to offer a perfect harmony and ultimately become a real family for the newcomers.

THREE COUNTRIES OPT OUT OF ECOWAS

In January 2025, three West African countries decided to withdraw from the Economic Community of West African States (ECOWAS), a regional political and economic union comprising fifteen West African countries. ECOWAS was founded in May 1975 in Lagos, Nigeria, and its creation inspired hope and had a Pan-African vision. Collectively, that entity comprises an area of 5,114,162 km² with an estimated population of over 424.34 million.

The organization aims to ensure the free movement of people and goods, and also encourages the establishment of best practices and implements policies like economic self-sufficiency, good education and health facilities, as well as principles of democracy, the rule of law, and the existence of good governance. ECOWAS has specialized agencies mandated to help the institution fulfill its mission: The West African Health Organization (WAHO), the West African Monetary Agency (WAMA), and many others.

A series of military coups occurred in West Africa between 2020 and 2023. It started in Mali, and gradually reached Burkina Faso and Niger. Other French-speaking countries experienced military takeovers, but the coups that were followed by a drastic break from the former colonial power, France, are the coups that occurred in the three countries mentioned above. These coups were real social movements that conveyed the concern, aspiration, and preoccupation of the masses. Certain features are common to these 3 countries: they are facing terrorist attacks, each of them is a Sahelian former French colony, they are classified among the poorest countries in the world, and they struck up a solid cooperation with Russia after booting France out. Those at the forefront of these political changes that affected the geopolitical dynamics of the world assert that the collaborations with Russia are strictly a win-win situation. Weapons are purchased from Russia, not acquired as a gift, and if Russian companies want to operate mining companies in Africa, the usual taxes and costs have to be paid.

A careful glance at the general situation in West Africa over the years reveals that ECOWAS has failed, to a large extent. In other words, the organization's attitude is contrary to what is stipulated as its missions and duties. The practice of democracy and good governance was never the concern of ECOWAS, and that explains the preponderance of rigged presidential elections and other scandalous scenarios that mar the political scene in many West African nations: real democracy is quasi-nonexistent. One frequently reads political comments that pose, with enough proof, that dictators who openly and blatantly violate[ed] the tenets of democracy are presidents within the ECOWAS sphere. Some of such heads of state are often referred to as "those who bayonet their own people". Another factor that weakens the West African institution is the large number of coup makers who rule over nations: Military strong presidents pose as civilians and get elected as democratic leaders within ECOWAS. Likewise, wealthy civilians perfectly plan and finance coups that overthrow and often kill their rivals or leaders who do not approve of their ideology. The principle of mutual support or aid is ignored at a moment like the current situation: no military assistance was provided to any of the countries that are currently being severely hit by terrorists; no aid has been allocated by ECOWAS to the millions of displaced persons within ECOWAS sub-regions.

The rule of law is not a reality within ECOWAS either: Citizens are harassed or maltreated in any attempt to cross into a neighboring country, and the gaping corruption is the antithesis of the rule of law. These weaknesses of the organization were pinpointed several years ago by Captain Thomas Sankara, who was president of Burkina Faso in 1984, during the 7th conference of the heads of state and governments in Lome, Togo. He surprised others with a different speech that recommended a combat against the former colonizer turned imperialist over time, stressing the link between economic development and the fight for economic liberation. That speech was a "big first one", which stood against the traditional pro-Western talks that implicitly asserted the submission of West African states to the European powers. Coincidentally, 40 years after that speech, Captain Ibrahim Traoré, the current president of Burkina Faso, put into practice what Sankara preached in Lome in 1984. Moreover, two other military rulers in countries that share a border with Burkina Faso are Traoré's staunch allies in this denunciation of ECOWAS. Burkina Faso, Mali, and Niger decided to leave ECOWAS after they coalesced into a three-nation union called the Union of Sahelian States (AES).

These three countries separately assert the power that they represent if they unite: Enormous, diverse mineral and other natural resources, a big and vibrant market, one common feeling, that of patriotism and anti-subjugation, the application of self-sufficiency, and the freedom to choose one's allies. It therefore does not come as a surprise when each of those countries chose to have a strong cooperation with Russia. Presidents Traoré, Goita and Tchiani respectively of Burkina, Mali and Niger are confident that the newly emerged union, the AES is working to install the same vision, in their societies, one of patriotism, a conviction that nothing remains as it was before, people's consciences are being whipped up and they are convinced that their country is all they have and is endowed enough to guarantee their survival and as a result, terrorists should not be allowed to take over any part of the country. Certain sources have it that the AES has already solved the challenge of the new common currency, once the economy and finance ministers and other influential personalities of the three countries met several times. Most media outlets in Burkina Faso and conversations with many Burkinabè reveal that all the technical aspects that come with the creation of such a union are being taken care of.

The main concern remains the following one: Certain fears are alleviated when one notices that despite the exit the of three countries, the overage citizen in the AES keep circulating easily out of the AES space The leaders of the new union pose that the union is a Pan-Africanist body (we are leaving ECOWAS, but we remain Pan-Africanists, they say). AES is so far self-sufficient at all levels, and the other or remaining countries of the ECOWAS are working to keep their economies sound without AES. AES citizens are able to reside and work in the space of the new and depleted ECOWAS. Most of the efforts are now geared towards appeasing people and urging them in this new onward march. Some degree of silence is kept around such details, and people are told not to worry an inch. The procedure in such a separation from a coalition is to write a letter voicing the intention of breaking away, and wait for a reply, which might take about a year to come out. The country members of AES have written a letter to ECOWAS, and no response has been received yet. Many historic events occurred in West Africa over the last four years, and more seem to be on their way.

THE HIDDEN SIDES AND REPERCUSSIONS OF SPORT: THE 2022 AFCON AND THE RUMBLE IN THE JUNGLE

The African Cup of Nations (AFCON) can now be referred to as the biggest and regular soccer event on the continent. As a biennial, it is hosted every other year, and this year's edition bears the name '2022 AFCON' because of the change that the COVID-19 pandemic threw into the calendar of the tournament. One does not have to be a rocket scientist to realize that the Cup was being used as a special socio-political 'tool or device'. We commonly hear of the politics of sport or national politics and sport. The correlation stems from the fact that sport competition or any entertainment works in favor of a leader whose power, popularity, and performance in his/her country is ailing. Such events lead the nationals to forget the problems of the nation for some time. All the energy and attention of the whole country, in that case, is geared toward the unfolding spectacle. Sport or Showbiz, therefore, works like 'the opium of the masses', to borrow Marx's terms. So, as long as the entertainment event is running in the country, a sense of patriotism 'glues' all nationals together: They believe that they have to play well and defend the honor of the nation, or for a great period, their focus, attention, and interest are all invested in the competition or performance.

Mobutu Sese Seko of Zaire (today's Democratic Republic of Congo) played that card in October 1974 with what is called "the Rumble in the jungle", the heavyweight championship boxing match between two African Americans, the undefeated and undisputed heavyweight champion George Foreman and Mohammad Ali (formerly Cassius Clay) before he converted to Islam after 1961.

With an attendance of 60,000 people, the event was one of the most-watched televised events at the time. It was watched by one billion television viewers around the world. Some arguably call it the greatest sporting event of the 20th century. In the field of boxing, that fight remains special; it marks the birth of the rope-a-dope tactic, introduced by Ali. The technique allows one contender to lean against the ropes of the boxing ring and draw non-injurious offensive punches, letting the opponent tire himself out. That gives the opportunity to the former to then execute devastating offensive punches and increase his chance of winning. The outcome of this specific match was a major upset; Ali, the underdog, won against Foreman by knockout in the 8th round.

The boxing match was the facade of an important political project: Fred Weymar, an American advisor to the then Zaire's president Mobutu Sese Seko, persuaded the latter that the publicity which such a high-profile event would generate would help his regime and make him more popular. Mobutu hosted that event to divert the focus of a nation that would see in him a more popular leader after the boxing match.

The incongruity of the event was shocking at first: Why should such a contest be hosted by an African country that is facing more burning existential challenges? For a while, Zaire hosted the two champions, their managers, and the side attractions of the boxing match, and in this case, several prominent African American stars flew to Kinshasa, the capital city of Zaire, to display their skills alongside the boxing match. The media coverage did not falter at all. Don King arranged the fight with music businessman Jerry Masucci, who took his record label's showcase group, the Fania All-Stars, to play at the venue. Still, to produce a real 'show within a show', a three-night-long music festival to hype the fight, Zaire 74, took place as scheduled, on September 22–24, including performances by James Brown, Celia Cruz and the Fania All-Stars, B.B. King, Miriam Makeba, The Spinners, Bill Withers, The Crusaders, and Manu Dibango, as documented in the 2008 film *Soul Power*.

So in 1974, A Rumble in the Jungle played the anesthetic effect that it was expected to have. Unlike before, a positive 'Papa Mobutu' figure replaced the Mobutu from whom people were making various demands. During the boxing competition, only positive vibrations took hold of the country. The president reached his ultimate goal, which was to buy time but diverting people's attention from the national malaise and get more time to devise strategies and confront the multi-pronged flail in the diseased nation, the common feature of newly 'independent' countries. This example and many others initiated the concept of 'politics and /or sport' in countries faced with serious challenges.

The Ivorian President Alassane OUATTARA is currently caught up in a complicated political situation, both at the national, sub-regional, and international levels. Many Ivorians are not happy because he violated the constitution and had himself re-elected for a third term in 2020. The fracture in his camp is not making things easier. His young, charismatic ally, Guillaume SORO, severed ties with Ouattara and is getting close to the West African countries that recently experienced coups. He visited the leaders of Burkina, Niger, and Mali and made a 'coded' statement that can be interpreted in many ways. Indeed, Mr. Soro, who was sentenced to life in prison for trying to stand in the way of President Ouattara, told the media that the time has come for him to put an end to his exile; he is back in Africa. Not much is said about his current address or location, which is another uncertainty that President Ouattara must handle. It might help to remind people of the large number of followers that the young dissident has.

At the international level, the Ivorian President meddled in actions and decisions that made him stand as a stooge of Western powers, especially France. He tirelessly defends the interests of France on the continent, through political bodies like ECOWAS. His quick and firm condemnation of the coups in Mali, Burkina, and Niger proved, according to many analysts, that he was "remote controlled". That tarnished his reputation in the West African sub-region as well as his country, where some people (although not so many in Côte d'Ivoire) applaud the coups and the anti-France decisions and measures. It therefore does not come as a surprise when Côte d'Ivoire campaigned hard to host the Cup of Nations this year. The budget allocated to the game is astronomical; the Cup became the dream of the whole nation. The national bad governance and other sources of malcontentment were forgotten overnight, at least for some weeks. It is recorded that out of a total cost of €1.5 billion, over €762 million was invested in infrastructure, and four stadiums were built, two others were extensively renovated, twenty-four training pitches were fitted, and several roads were modernized or extended. The other part of the equation is that one and a half million visitors were expected during the competition, and Côte d'Ivoire is hoping to reap the economic benefits of the investments made for the occasion.

Now that the host country has won the cup after 40 years of waiting, other financial benefits might be obtained. This financial calculation does not come as a surprise since President Ouattara is known as a competent and experienced economist. The host country might recoup the money invested, but what is certain is that for weeks or months, no political crisis will be mentioned in the country. For people who are known as party and fun lovers, this victory will simply compound merry-making. A two-day holiday was declared right after the Elephants (the national team) won the trophy, and the national feeling is one of joy and happiness. President Alassane Dramane Ouattara was then revered as "Papa ADO"; the initials in his name are used to call him "the father of the nation". This sentiment is far from the pre-Cup feeling of socio-political tension and serious dissensions over the management of the economy.

President Ouattara seems to have used the traditional magic of sport and entertainment to alleviate tension during difficult times. The trouble has been swept under the carpet. How long will it take for these disagreements to resurface? They certainly will not remain silent for a long time. On a more personal level, Ivorians need to learn the art of playing a game. Soccer is a game, entertainment, despite the financial rewards that come with victory. Vehicles and loads of properties were vandalized at some point during this cup, and about 20 years ago, lives were cruelly lost when a neighboring country beat Côte d'Ivoire in a soccer match.

APARTHEID IS BACK IN CERTAIN PARTS OF SOUTH AFRICA

Very few youngsters today know what "Apartheid" means, and although some of them claim to have heard the name Nelson Mandela, they do not know much about the man. Apartheid is a system of racial discrimination/segregation that was unique to South Africa and was imposed by the white Europeans who settled there in 1652. This system divided the people and labeled them as whites and non-whites based on their skin color. Apartheid, which in Afrikaans, one of the official languages in South Africa, is derived from Dutch and means "apartness", a policy that governed relations between South Africa's white minority and nonwhite majority for much of the latter half of the 20th century, and it imposed racial segregation and political and economic discrimination against nonwhites. Although the legislation that formed the foundation of apartheid had been repealed by the early 1990s, the social and economic repercussions of the discriminatory policy persisted into the 21st century. A little research into History reveals these key facts: Racial segregation, sanctioned by law, was widely practiced in South Africa before 1948. With time, it was extended and given the name "Apartheid". The implementation of this "separate development" since the 1960s was made possible through the Population Registration Act of 1950, which classified all South Africans as either Bantu (all Black Africans), Colored (those of mixed race), or white. A fourth category—Asian (Indian and Pakistani)—was later added. One of the other most significant acts in terms of forming the basis of the apartheid system was the Group Areas Act of 1950. It established residential and business sections in urban areas for each race, and members of other races were barred from living, operating businesses, or owning land in them, which led to thousands of Colored, Blacks, and Indians being removed from areas classified for white occupation. In practice, this act and two others (adopted in 1913 and 1955) had the following consequences that will fundamentally determine the tune of life in South Africa for decades. More than 80 percent of South Africa's land became the property by the white minority. To help enforce the segregation of the races and prevent Blacks from encroaching on white areas, the government strengthened the existing "pass" laws, which required nonwhites to carry documents authorizing their presence in restricted areas. Other acts also led to the physical separation of the races. Separate educational standards were established for nonwhites. State-run schools were established, and Black children were required to attend them; the goal was to train the children for the manual labor and menial jobs that the government deemed suitable for those of their race. The Extension of University Education Act was passed in 1959 and prohibited "established universities" from accepting nonwhite students. "Ethnic university colleges were founded for Coloreds, Indians, Zulus, and students from other ethnic groups, as well as a medical school for Blacks. Almost the whole world condemned Apartheid, except countries like Israel and Côte d'Ivoire (the latter maintained at least commercial ties with South Africa during Apartheid).

Racial segregation was also practiced in the United States, and the term was mainly used there in reference to the legally or socially enforced separation of African Americans from whites, as well as the separation of other ethnic minorities from the majority and mainstream communities. It was called "Jim Crow" and had the same features as Apartheid in South Africa. It is generally said that racial discrimination in the US was outlawed by the Civil Rights Act of 1964, but the phenomenon is more complex, and the focus of this reflection is the case of South Africa.

As one can expect in such cases, there is always some opposition, and there was always some opposition to apartheid within South Africa. Black African groups, with the support of some whites, held demonstrations and strikes, and there were many instances of violent protest and sabotage. One of the first—and most violent—demonstrations against apartheid took place in Sharpeville on March 21, 1960; the police response was to open fire, killing about 69 Black Africans and wounding many more. The Soweto—a township of the City of Johannesburg Municipality- uprising (or Soweto riots) was a series of demonstrations and protests led by black school children that began on 16 June 1976. Students from various schools began to protest in the streets of Soweto in response to the introduction of Afrikaans as the medium of instruction in black schools. It is estimated that 20,000 students took part in the protests. They were met with fierce police brutality, and many were shot and killed. The number of pupils killed in the uprising is usually estimated as 176, but some sources estimate as many as 700 fatalities.

The main organization against this racial decimation was the African National Congress (ANC), founded on 8 January 1912 in Bloemfontein by Walter Rubusana, Sol Plaatje, John Dube, and several others. In 1944, a left-wing youth League was formed with activists like Walter Sisulu, Nelson Mandela, and Oliver Tambo.

Lawyer Nelson Mandela was shortly appointed as the leader of one of the Youth League of the ANC. He was repeatedly arrested and then was sentenced in 1952 to life imprisonment for conspiring to overthrow the state. He served 27 years in prison. Amid growing domestic and international pressure, he was released in 1990. In 1994, the multiracial general election was held. Mandela led the ANC to victory and became president. He led a broad coalition government which promulgated a new constitution and emphasized reconciliation. Mandela stayed in power from 1994 to 1999; he passed in 2013. The sacrifices and battles of Mandela and the ANC was aiming at bringing racial equality, stamping out racially motivated violence, and securing prosperity for all.

What is scary these days is to find out that some nostalgics who are still attached to the Apartheid era have created their own "whites only" communities, isolated from Blacks and Coloreds, whom, in their words, they cannot stand. How wide will these communities grow, and what will they generate? What do they represent in a post-apartheid era? Orania City (in the Northern Cape) is one of such communities. It is a real enclave for Afrikaners, with 1,600 inhabitants, and children are taught only Afrikaner in school, the language of the Dutch settlers. When the government took the land away from whites, there was compensation, but the Oranians suspect that a new phase of land re-appropriation will take place, and this time, whites will not be compensated. It is therefore a stronghold of Apartheid and Afrikaner culture, nostalgic people, and in schools, 2 curricula are taught: the national one, and that of the enclave, where there is no mention of personalities like Nelson Mandela. The question that pops up here is: are these cities a sign of nostalgia for apartheid or the reflection of an unease among Afrikaners today? Some of the whites justify their relocation to such areas with the laws aiming to increase black employment that have ultimately turned against white South Africans, who, by default, lose their jobs. High crime rates in other parts of the country are also mentioned as reasons behind the establishment of such enclaves. "I like the vibration here. We set a good example for other parts of the country; we are more focused here, with fewer crimes. We are still part of the broader community; we do not feel isolated," is what some residents say. Orania has its own currency, the Ora.

Kleinfontein, which is located 30 kilometers south of Pretoria, on the other hand, is a more radical segregated white town. It was founded in 1992, has 1,300 residents who aim at creating an independent state where Blacks are not accepted because they are violent and "less civilized," as Ronelle Berrington, the CEO and founder of the community, says. The residents of Kleinfontein are convinced that a civil war is about to break out between blacks and whites, and they remain ever-ready for that clash. They stipulate that their other motives are to preserve their language and culture. "We are a cultural minority that the Rainbow nation is driving to extinction, and we are combating that", some of them say. Balmoral is the third whites-only town. One wonders if Apartheid is not gradually coming back in South Africa.

THE BELGIAN COLONIZATION OF CONGO: THE MOST ATROCIOUS EUROPEAN ADVENTURE

The Berlin Conference of 1884-1885 decreed the division of Africa among Western countries after missionaries were sent to Africa, as explorers first. The task these ones were assigned was to discover the wealth of the continent so that a map of Africa could be provided to the Westerners, who would use it during the Berlin Conference. The lion's share fell into the hands of Britain, probably because of the mercantilist mind and culture. The French were second, and then the Spanish, Portuguese, and Germans had their share of "the cake" too. European colonization came with violence, and certain colonizers were generally known to be more violent than others. Sources point to the Belgian colonization of the Congo as the most brutal and cruel one. Congo was called the Free State of the Congo at the Berlin Conference. So, King Leopold II of Belgium was granted total sovereignty over that territory, which he ruled as his private property until 1908, when he passed it into the hands of the Belgian state. Rather than control the Congo as a colony, as other European powers did throughout Africa, Leopold privately owned the region. My position is that none of these rules is justifiable and "clean". They are all exploitative and bloody, but that of King Leopold stands out because of its gluttony and brutality.

Two eras characterize the encounter of Congo with Belgium: King Leopold II's rule of the Free Land of the Congo from 1885 to 1908, and that of the Belgian Congo that followed, from 1908 to 1960. A document stands out in History and is generally referred to as King Leopold's Letter to Colonial Missionaries (1883). It was the missive he gave to the missionaries before they set off to Africa. Many academics have read that letter and have copies, and it opens with these lines that capture its essence:

"Reverends, Fathers and Dear Compatriots: The task that is given to fulfill is very delicate and requires much tact. You will go certainly to evangelize, but your evangelization must inspire above all Belgian interests. Your principal objective in our mission in the Congo is never to teach the niggers to know God, this they know already. They speak and submit to a Mungu, one Nzambi, one Nzakomba, and what else I don't know. They know that to kill, to sleep with someone else's wife, to lie, and to insult is bad. Have the courage to admit it; you are not going to teach them what they know already. Your essential role is to facilitate the task of administrators and industrials, which means you will go to interpret the gospel in a way it will be best to protect your interests in that part of the world. For these things, you have to keep watch on disinteresting our savages from the richness that is plenty [in their underground. To avoid that, they get interested in it, and make you murderous] competition and dream one day to overthrow you".

Kenyan Ngũgĩ wa Thiong'o writes, referring to the same deceit (with humor added) that the white man asked Africans to close their eyes and pray. Blacks then closed their eyes so tight and "prayed" and when they opened their eyes, their land was taken away from them. The same writer goes further to say that "the Bible paved the way for the sword". King Philippe, the Belgian current ruler, traveled to the Congo in 2020 and tried to express his regrets for the conduct of his ancestors in today's Democratic Republic of the Congo, which was King Leopold's Congo. That gesture did not go down well with the Congolese, and general opinion sees in King Philippe's words a twisted and improper action that falls way short of a sincere regret and a real apology. The press captured the Belgian King's attitude in these terms: "Belgium's King Philippe has not apologized for the exploitation, racism, and acts of violence during his country's colonization of the Democratic Republic of the Congo (DRC). Rather, he chose to convey his "deepest regrets" for the colonial humiliation and punishment meted out to the Congolese people".

King Leopold II had carved his private colony out of 100 km² of Central African rainforest by claiming to protect the "natives" from Arab slavers. Though the territory was governed from Brussels, the administrative capital was the port city of Boma, from where the massive exports of raw materials were shipped. Boma was the residence of the Governor General, who was appointed by the Belgian King, to whom he was directly answerable. As stated earlier, an apologia is always needed in such cases of deceit and exploitation, and paternalism was used to justify such ownership. Colonial Congo was therefore labeled a fiefdom, which was baptized the Congo Free State. The profits from that land were for King Leopold and also Belgium. Hence, the interchangeable use of the 2 periods.

According to some estimates, killings, famine, and disease caused the deaths of up to 10 million Congolese during just the first 75 years of Belgian (general) rule from 1885 to 1960. That "special colony" was turned into a massive labor camp, and made a big fortune for Belgium from the harvest of wild rubber. Belgium put in place the machinery required for a thorough and unimaginable brutal exploitation. There was a regime of terror, mass killings, and, of course, amputations. During the Belgian rule, the population of the Congo dwindled by half, to 10 million.

The timber, gold, diamond, and other invaluable mineral resources extorted from certain colonized lands like the Gold Coast made the industrial revolution possible in Britain in the 19th century. Some Afrocentric scholars put it that if colonization had not befallen Africa, this continent would have been far ahead of Europe today. Cheikh Anta Diop is one of such erudite persons, and he bases his statement on scientific data, not emotion and unmeasurable stuff. Britain does not have any natural resources apart from coal and the sea (for fishing and hydroelectricity). The plundered resources from the "British Empire" enabled the industrial take-off of Cecile Rhodes's country. Walter Rodney summarizes all this in his seminal book *How Europe Underdeveloped Africa* (1972). In the specific case of the Congo, the rubber harvest directly contributed to Belgium's rising economic power. This again confirms that what belonged to King Leopold was also Belgian property. Ivory was equally one of the precious materials the Congo offered. The colonial policy in the Congo was so cruel that one finds it difficult to render in words what was meted out to Africans there: At the end of the day, after long hours of forced labor in the rubber plantations, fathers, mothers and children were lined up behind their rubber harvest of the day; that was weighed by colonial agents and a minimum weight had to be reached by everybody, that weight or quantity was called "quota"(s). Whoever fell short of that quantity had one hand chopped off. If the following day the same person did not meet that minimum, their second hand was amputated, and then the process continued. People were raped and tormented by colonial agents. It is reported that those who resisted King Leopold's orders, or those who refused and wouldn't comply, had their hands and feet cut off, and even the children and wives of the men who couldn't meet their "quotas" met the same fate. That horrible chopping or amputation, and other torments were used to silence people into total submission. Cutting the limbs of Africans was such a central symbol in Belgian colonization: it signified the superiority of whites over Africans, and it also meant fidelity to the King. Colonial auxiliaries quelled agitations or anti-colonial movements or sentiments, and they had to prove that they were not wasting precious bullets, and to do that, they had to bring to their superiors the amputated hand of any rebellious Congolese whom they killed. What is referred to today as the crimes of Belgium or the Belgian Congo genocide started in 1885, and French-born British journalist Edmund Dene Morel was the first to draw the world's attention to that brutal exploitation. He revealed photos of forced labor, murders, child soldiers, homeless people, torture, and genocide in the Congo. Then writers Mark Twain in "King Leopold's Soliloquy" (1905) and Joseph Conrad were critical voices who revealed the atrocities being inflicted on the Congolese people. In 1905, after several months of investigation, a commission published a report that corroborated the abuses that had been denounced. The Belgian king was finally forced to renounce his rule over the Free State of the Congo, which subsequently became a colony of Belgium, and was duly renamed the Belgian Congo. Nonetheless, between 1885 and 1960 (the year of independence), History records that King Leopold II ruled the Congo. The atrocities might have reduced or not, although there is no documentation to that effect, and it does not come as a surprise when, in 2020, King Leopold II's statue was removed by protesters from a public square in the city of Antwerp in Belgium during worldwide protests against the West's racist colonial past.

THE TRUTH AT LAST! COMPAORÉ CHARGED WITH SANKARA'S DEATH

On the Burkinabè political scene, the main news these days is the indictment of former President Blaise Compaoré for the assassination of his brother-in-arms and former President, Thomas Sankara. Graffiti calling for Justice for Sankara is a common sight in Ouagadougou. Thomas Sankara was in power from 1983 to 1987, and during his tenure, the country experienced more development than in all the previous thirty-four years of neocolonial civilian and military rule. Thomas Sankara was called the "Che Guevara" of Africa because of his military attire (beret with a star), his fiery speeches, and remarkable energy. Between 1983 and 1987, Burkina Faso underwent significant progress: schools and hospitals were built, and citizens were vaccinated against deadly diseases. Corruption was reduced. Women empowerment was also a central part of his reforms. A Pan-Africanist, Sankara followed a Marxist/Leninist path, which gained him both supporters and opponents. While figures like Jerry John Rawlings of Ghana and Fidel Castro of Cuba embraced him as the young, passionate comrade of the global revolutionary movement, other Presidents, such as Moussa Traoré of Mali, Félix H. Boigny of Côte d'Ivoire, and François Mitterrand of France, saw his ideological stance as threatening. These right-wing African leaders viewed him as a danger. Due to his charisma, they feared his rising influence could inspire young soldiers in their armies to overthrow them.

The Murder of Sankara, and the Burkina Revolution

Unfortunately, the metamorphosis of the Burkina society abruptly came to an end in the afternoon of October 1987 when a commando, carrying out the orders of Blaise Compaoré, gunned down Thomas Sankara along with many of his co-workers and his security. It was a real betrayal, since Sankara and Compaoré shared a friendship as brothers. Blaise had allegedly been adopted by Sankara's family; the two young men had trained in military academies. Compaoré was Minister of Justice under Sankara. He was also the second in command, although there was no constitutional provision for one. Compaoré was a major figure in the coup d'état that brought Sankara to power in August 1983.

On April 13th, 2021, a court indicted Blaise Compaoré in connection with the 1987 murder of Thomas Sankara. A statement issued by the court cited "complicity in assassination" and an "attack on state security" by Compaoré. Thirteen other soldiers were also indicted and charged with assassination and concealment of corpses. The fallen heroes of October 15th, 1987, had been hurriedly buried in a mass grave, and later, when civil society put pressure on Compaoré's regime, a somewhat befitting burial was given to them at the Dagnoen cemetery in Ouagadougou. After an autopsy, Sankara's widow, Mariam, revealed that his body was riddled with more than a dozen bullets. The Sankara's lawyer, Bénéwendé Stanislas, saw Compaoré's inculpation as a move in the right direction.

The Catalyst of Justice

The civil society in Burkina Faso is largely credited with the indictment of Compaoré. It has remained alert to governance and justice since its participation in the ousting of Compaoré. This also led to the establishment of the Ministry of National Reconciliation by Compaoré's successor, Rock Marc Christian Kaboré.

Compaoré has been living in Côte d'Ivoire, and this indictment is supposed to pressure the Ivorian government to extradite him to Burkina to face trial. However, there are a couple of concerns: How will Compaoré's return affect the political terrain in Burkina Faso? Will it have any impact on the current terrorist attacks bedeviling the country? However, these questions can only be answered if Compaoré is extradited, which is a slim possibility because there is no extradition treaty between the two countries. In addition, Compaoré has been a longtime ally of the Ivorian President, Alassane Ouattara. He is known to have provided support to Ouattara during the 2010 elections that led to civil war in Côte d'Ivoire. The alliance between Compaoré and Ouattara is evident in the conscription of a large number of Burkinabè young men who went to northern Côte d'Ivoire to fight on the rebels' side; they were in support of Mr. Ouattara. It is also not a secret that many of those rebels who fought against the then-President Laurent Gbagbo were trained in Burkinabè territory. In addition to this, Compaoré's wife, Chantal, is Ivorian. Compaoré has therefore found refuge with his in-laws and the man whom he helped to gain power. These factors cast doubts on the possibility of an extradition of Compaoré to face trial in Burkina Faso. The final ruling in the case of Thomas Sankara's assassination was the condemnation in absentia in 2022 of Compaoré to life imprisonment. Some of his acolytes were sentenced to imprisonment for a period ranging from 3 to 20 years.

RECOLONIZATION OF THE DEMOCRATIC REPUBLIC OF CONGO: THE RULE OF CHINA AND THE US

The power of China in the world in general and developing countries in particular is not anything new anymore. The Chinese are now having their turn in the colonization process in the world. What European powers did in the 19th century, after the Berlin Conference of 1884, unleashed the possession of Africa by Europe, a phenomenon that was simply termed colonization. Very few nations in Africa, Asia, and the Americas escaped that subjugation. In Africa, only Ethiopia and Liberia were not colonized, and in Southeast Asia, the French and the British failed after numerous attempts. The Thai people love their sovereignty so much that they preferred to let go of a portion of their territory to France, to remain free. That explains why Laos became a French protectorate and then colony between 1893 and 1953, and Thailand never experienced colonization.

Needless to repeat that colonization brought upon Africa all types of exploitation, humiliation, and destruction of the nation's ego. The natural resources were pillaged and enabled the industrial take-off of Western countries like the UK, a country whose resources are coal and the sea only, and used the mineral and other natural resources of its colonies to kick-start their industrial revolution. In the same vein, France, which produces no gold, happens to have a large repository of gold that comes from its colonies; it contributes to tying those countries economically to France. Colonization made scholars like the Guianese Walter Rodney utter seminal statements like: "Africa developed Europe at the same rate that Europe underdeveloped Africa". China was not a superpower when Europe was at the peak of its domination in the world. China was busy drafting development plans and strategies during that period. Chiang Kai-shek, Mao Zedong, and other leaders with vision were working to establish a road map that would lead to the repositioning of China, from the margin to the center.

The power that China gained is now being used for Chinese colonization in the world. Every nation owes China in one way or another. The US takes into consideration the economic and geopolitical weight of only one nation: China. But what China is doing these days is a special colonization that deserves serious thinking. The rule of that country over nations whose natural and human potential she covets is multifaceted and complicated. The whole world seems to watch, in a state of powerlessness, the progress of Chinese hegemony, which has, among others, cultural negative effects on the countries that are victims: an example is the Chinese instructor who was seen in an African country teaching children extremely self-deprecating sentences and phrases in a video in February 2020. Teaching the Chinese language for free and allocating scholarships to students in Africa and other developing continents to train in China is a new and strong educational and cultural phenomenon. What makes this Chinese domination special is the following: the unfair, unjust, near-slavery form that it takes, coupled with the neutralization of the governing system and powers, especially in the case of Africa. An observation that perfectly illustrates the real color of Chinese hegemony is the case of the Democratic Republic of Congo (DRC) and the firm power that China imposes over this country, in the exploitation of the mineral resources of the country. That is the picture provided by an observation from a certain angle. But the truth is that China has fully opened its markets to Africa, to export and feed the Chinese. But sadly enough, Africans are not using that opportunity enough.

We could start by pointing out that the DRC is known to have the most precious mineral resources of the world and 2 factors also emerge in this case: the US is losing her grip over several countries to China, and strangely enough, a mineral-rich country like the DRC has a population that lives in utter misery: The Democratic Republic of Congo is torn between war camps, and the fertile lands of the country are left untouched since most citizens prefer to migrate to the cities (of the DRC or neighboring countries) to sell their skills and use their income for a luxurious life style which is fake, a real case of saddening verisimilitude that leaves many development experts aghast. When one decides to discover, find, or experience the natural riches of the DRC, this is what the trajectory of that mission would be: You might want to start your journey from the mountains of North Kivu, where the mines of Rubaya are, in a very beautiful area called Masisi. The next mines, still in the same area, are called the "Mines of Walikale," and there, one comes face-to-face with the untouchable power of an American mining company, *Alphamine,* that usurps the governance of all the Congolese institutions. An authorization of the presidency of the country and all the institutions that regulate the mining sector, plus the presence of some MPs and a flight in a national airplane, do not grant access to the site. That makes you wonder what the American company has to hide and also leads one to accept the information that contends that in those mines, Americans extract gold, tin, cassiterite which is the source of tin metal, coltan, a heat-resistant powder that can store electrical charge and niobium, a very rare and special mineral used in the stabilization of rockets.

The company is accountable to nobody, although it is situated on Congolese territory, with its airstrip, the highest Congolese authorities are not welcome there. Moving forward, it might be difficult to access North Kivu, an area under siege and ruled by a sovereign military governor whose status is close to that of a king. These 2 cases blatantly undermine the concept or idea of an independent DRC. Then, moving to South Kivu, one finds the Lihuhu mines, in the Kabare territory, nestled in a breathtakingly beautiful environment. Unfortunately, modern-day slavery is present; workers were made to dig profound holes on a surface situated at an altitude of 2,200 meters, where only heather grows. From Bukavu, the capital city of that area, the next place to visit in such a mission should be the mining area of Kamituga. Due to the insecurity on the roads in that war-torn country, little airplanes are the means of transportation. But a plane cannot land in that mining area without the authorization of the Chinese. There is, therefore, a Chinese territory in the Democratic Republic of Congo. The most baffling aspect is that no one knows what minerals are extracted there, what the quantity is, or what is done in the area. The Nobel Peace Laureate Denis Mukwege laments the fact that the Chinese trade in gold by selling it on the black market, under the protection of their militia. Nobody can say for sure where they get the authorization from. So, they pay no tax and pocket the dollars they get from the sales and leave. Moving further, one lands at Kitutu's little airport. The surprise there is the fact that the Chinese demolished the road leading to the mine, making it impossible to access the site without their control or agreement. The mining area is labelled as a "non-authorized" one, belonging to a Chinese company whose name remains secret. A phone call from the Minister in charge of the mines cannot move the Chinese, and one still remains trapped, aloof from the mines. Such a phone would even warrant only one thing: the Chinese closing all their offices, doors, gates, and vanishing (temporarily, of course) from the scene. Be it journalists, tourists, or ministers, access to the site is not granted. So, there is no doubt that the Congolese government is part of this problem. They feed into this system.

All this is revolting, according to the famous international Cameroonian-born political scientist and journalist Alain FOKA, who asks the younger generation of Africans not to repeat the mistake made by their seniors, which is to remain amorphous and watch foreign companies pillage all the natural resources of the nation, with no respect for countries that are said to be independent.

BURKINA FASO IN THE AFRICAN PERSPECTIVE

Burkina Faso means the country of the incorruptible person, a name coined from two main languages of the country (Moshi and Jula), and that name replaced the neocolonial name of the country, Upper Volta. Burkina Faso is a French-speaking former French colony in West Africa. It is a landlocked country surrounded by Togo, Benin, Ghana, Côte d'Ivoire, Niger, and Mali. The population of the country is about 20 million, and the vegetation is the savannah. The country has two seasons: a rainy season that lasts from June to October and a dry season that runs from November to May. The main activity in the country is agriculture, which generally yields the following: corn, millet, beans, rice, and cotton. The latter is the main product that the country exports, besides cow meat and gold, which has been discovered recently in Burkina. The currency is the CFA franc (Communauté Financière d'Afrique). The land mass is 274,200 sq km (105,870 sq miles). The main languages spoken in Burkina are Moshi, followed by Jula, and Fulani or Fulfulde; French was the official language until the regime of Captain Ibrahim Traoré demoted its status and uplifted national languages. So national languages (Mooré also called Moshi, Jula also known as Wangara, Fulfuldé or Fulani and Bissa / Bisa sometimes referred to as the "Bissa or Bussanga Language" are the official languages of the country and French is the "Language of Work" alongside English since all official documents are still written in French. That change occurred in January 2024. The main religions are Islam, Catholicism, the protestant church, and Traditional African religion. Islam and Christianity are practiced by almost 98% of the population, and African traditional religion is practiced by 2% of the population, although Muslims and Christianity tend to also worship African gods. Life expectancy is 59 years (men) and 61 years (women).

Regarding History and the key events that are proper to Burkina, one can mention the following: in 1896, several kingdoms conglomerated as a French protectorate known as Upper Volta. Upper Volta became independent in 1960 with Maurice Yaméogo as its first president. He was later overthrown by the military, and a series of coups d'état were unleashed until 2015. Among the 5 coups d'état that the country experienced, from 1980 to 2015 (the total number of military take overs in the history of the country is 7), the most remarkable one is the 1983 coup that brought Captain Thomas Sankara to power. He took drastic measures that made the country change for the better. In a leftist model of governance called the August 4 Revolution, the economy of the country prospered, food self-sufficiency was one of the priorities, and healthcare was improved, civic education was inculcated in the overage Burkinabè (a native from Burkina, a name coined from the rules and structures of the third main language, Fulani). That explains why the name of the country was changed from the colonial name Upper Volta to Burkina Faso in 1984, to recapture the dignity of the people of that land. Thomas Sankara was murdered in a coup led by his friend and Minister Blaise Compaoré, who stayed in power for 25 years and ultimately was chased from power by a popular insurrection led by young people who had known only Blaise Compaoré as president. The latter sought refuge in neighboring Côte d'Ivoire, where he currently is. Then a civilian rule started, with Roch Marc Christian Kaboré, who was elected as President in 2015 and 2020. The current socio-economic and political situation of Burkina is the following:

terrorists attacks that have now drastically reduced, an economy which is prospering vertiginously, and a sense of civism that Sankara's rule ignited; that civism is being magnified by the current regime in power.

The terrorist attacks started around 2015, when Blaise Compaore was ousted from power by Civil Society. One of the reasons justifying the upsurge of terrorism after Blaise was forced out of power is the fact that Blaise Compaoré, who was a staunch ally of France (that sustained him in power for a quarter of a century and used him as the mediator in many conflicts in the sub-region), was cooperating with terrorists. Sources say that a group of terrorists were welcomed in Burkina Faso; they were indeed sent to Burkina by France, and the then Burkinabè president Compaoré welcomed them. When their host was forced out of power, President Kaboré, who succeeded him, refused to cooperate with the terrorists who suddenly lost the haven where they were. Then Blaise Compaoré allegedly pledged that Burkina Faso would not know peace as long as he is away. That was the prevailing socio political situation in the country for almost 10 years, until Captain Traoré seized power in September 2022. The terrorist attacks were so severe that certain parts of the country, like the Eastern area (Tougan), were qualified as red zones and travelers were advised not to venture there. President Kaboré was incapable in front of such a cascade of violence. The army was incapable of defeating these terrorists. The next piece will say more about those salient points raised here. It is important to bear in mind that these violent attacks were carried out by terrorists, not Jihadists.

A DIFFERENT FATE FOR AFRICAN CHILD SOLDIERS

Africa has known its fair share of civil wars, and unfortunately, that tragedy is going on to such an extent that the continent is associated with civil wars. Although some of these conflicts unfolded several years ago, like the Biafran War in Nigeria (1967-1970), most of them erupted around the mid-1980s, when the rush for mineral resources (an activity ignited mainly by Western capitalism) generated that cohort of cruelty, violence, massacre, and trauma in Africa. Liberia, Sierra Leone, Côte d'Ivoire, Rwanda, and, more recently, Ethiopia and Tigray are or were some of those "hot" zones in Africa. No one is spared, and people of all ages are involved in these wars where they kill or get killed. Adults, teenagers, and children are soldiers, men and women are fighters, or are used as weapons to intimidate rival camps. Rape is used as a weapon of war, and to crown it all, women and children are also made to carry loads (weapons, foodstuffs, and others) for the combatants most of the time. There is no doubt that the issue of child soldiers has been debated several times, at numerous fora; hence, some critics view discrimination in who is called a child soldier. Such people take into consideration the UN texts and their definition of who a child soldier is (any one below the age of 18 and recruited by an armed group to fight or aid in a fight); they further state that children were conscripted by Napoleon for his armies in France in 1814 and thousands of children participated on all sides in World War I and World War II and no mention is made of child soldiers in such cases. Eurocentric analysts would say that those are remote cases in History, but such a silence could also be justified by the power of Western hegemony. What cannot be denied is that seeing children deeply involved in armed conflicts is a painful sight, regardless of the country or conflict. In Africa, certain cases stand out, some are stories or cases of child soldiers who have been rescued and rehabilitated by international organizations like UNICEF, etc., while many others remain traumatized and live a complicated life of crime, addiction, sex trade, etc., things that they would not have done had they not been forcefully recruited into one of the fighting camps. One example of the first case is Ishmael Beah from Sierra Leone, who fought as a child soldier in his native country, killed people of all ages and genders, and saw his father, mother, and siblings executed. And he was then forced into the conflict as a child soldier at age 12. He went through a successful rehabilitation (with ups and downs, but it finally turned out to be a success), and an American lady adopted him. He subsequently migrated to the US, where he schooled, healed, and started a new and completely different life: he became an extraordinary motivational speaker who is adored by listeners whom he mesmerizes with the story of his life and with his mission as an advocate for the eradication of the child soldier phenomenon. What also adds to Mr. Beah's achievements is his famous best seller, *A Long Way Gone: The True Story of a Child Soldier* (2007), a memoir in which he recounts all the stages of his life as a child soldier. Readings and the media today reveal that not all child soldiers have such a successful "reconstruction" or improvement of their lives. Many are still battling with crippling vices, and one is forced to ask, "Why do these child soldiers remain caught up in such a vicious, pitiful cycle"? Are international organizations tired of rescuing child soldiers in Africa? Are the national authorities making enough effort for the child soldiers to receive help? Two examples of such a failure (Canadian General Roméo Dallaire, who was commander of the UN peacekeeping forces in Rwanda during the genocide, calls such a nonfeasance "the failure of humanity" in his memoir). One case that catches the reader's attention is the situation of child soldiers in Liberia. One often has the impression that not much is being done to assist the victims in that country. Two sad and telling examples are the following: the post-war life of a girl and a boy soldier. The first one narrates her ordeal this way: "When I was 14, I was forced out of school and onto the war camp by soldiers. I was put on the front line and had to fight; I killed many people and became addicted to drugs during the war. Now that the war has ended, I am still addicted to drugs, prostitute myself, attack and kill people to take their properties. We are receiving counseling from a UN-funded organization". Two points stand out here: a counselor who attends to this female child soldier laments the fact that although they are doing their best as counselors, these former child soldiers need a genuine counseling center, and a re-location that gives them decent accommodation and allows constant monitoring, two things that are highly needed since those who leave the counseling sessions always go back to their street life; the counselor then makes another poignant statement which is that they lack funding and she explains that there is not enough money to assist the child soldiers and help them achieve healing. As a result, such young people are called "zogo", a slur in Liberian society meaning that someone is a "good-for-nothing, unfit to be in a society". The young girl herself states that people like her need assistance from the government, to "flush the drugs out of our body so that I can return to where I was before the war". The statements of the counselor and the former child soldier indicate that international organizations are not allocating enough funds to the treatment of child soldiers in Liberia, and the

Liberian government is not pulling its weight, since it cannot provide these victims the treatment they need. The second example of the inadequacy of the assistance given to former child soldiers in Liberia is shown by the life of a young man, who is still "battling" the trauma engendered by his role in that war. He says, "I took away mothers', fathers', and children's lives". Reports from the WHO pose that more than 40% of people in Liberia live with Post Traumatic Stress Disorder (PTSD), more than 25,000 were killed, and less than 1% of those affected have access to mental health services. Sadly enough, many boy soldiers like the one whom we are mentioning here returned home, only to be ostracized by their families and communities. No demobilization and reintegration were attempted at the national level to give them a second chance in life, and they were stigmatized forever. The question that pops up here is: if the definition of a child soldier depends on the part of the globe one comes from, should the treatment of former child soldiers also be unequally implemented, depending on countries or periods (specific years)? Should such a primordial mission rely on the lousy policies of individual countries or international organizations?

POLITICS AND THE ELIMINATION OR SUDDEN DEATH OF COMRADES: BURKINA FASO AND CÔTE D'IVOIRE

One is dumfounded when we look at the political scene in Burkina Faso and in Côte d'Ivoire at a certain level. The former president of Burkina, Blaise Compaoré, and the current president of Côte d'Ivoire have lost very close allies or brothers in arms. While Compaoré was accused of killing his allies or ministers, Alassane Dramane Ouattara of Côte d'Ivoire is currently in the midst of turmoil: two of his prime ministers, Amadou Gon Coulibaly and Hamed Bakayogo, have died in 8 months. That led many observers to look at President Ouattara with suspicion. Did these two presidents, Compaoré and Ouattara, kill their allies?

The Burkina Faso Scenario

Blaise Compaoré became President in Burkina Faso after he sent a commando that was trained and faithful to him, the paratroopers of Pô, a city close to Ghana, to assassinate Thomas Sankara, who was like a brother to Compaoré: Sankara's parents had adopted Blaise as their son, and Sankara and Blaise trained in several military academies. In Burkina, they were always seen together; Blaise was a super minister: Minister of justice, with special functions at the presidency. He would have been called the prime minister had it been in a civilian regime. Then, on October 15th, 1987, Sankara was gunned down by soldiers who were executing the orders of Compaoré. After Sankara was eliminated, the other two members of the initial quaternion (Sankara, Compaoré, Henri Zongo, and

Lingani) were executed in 1989, for allegedly plotting to overthrow Compaoré. So after Captain Blaise Compaoré had Captain Sankara assassinated, barely two years later, he killed Captain Henry Zongo and Major Boukary J.B. Lingani. Compaoré then ruled Burkina for a quarter of a century, single-handedly. During his reign, several academics, leaders of students' unions, well-seasoned soldiers, and popular artists who were championing the cause of the downtrodden "disappeared". The truth is that they were all killed by Blaise's men because they were seen as threats to his stability and comfort. In October 2014, Compaoré was ousted by a popular insurrection and found exile in neighboring Côte d'Ivoire.

Historical Bond between Côte d'Ivoire and Burkina Faso

Côte d'Ivoire and Burkina Faso (called Upper Volta at that time) have a long history of cohabitation and common socio-political activities that all started during colonization, since the two countries were French colonies. Burkina Faso was used as a reservoir of workforce to supply workers in the coffee and cocoa plantations of Côte d'Ivoire, under the supervision of France. Roads, railways, and bridges were constructed by Burkinabè men so that the products and prduces in Côte d'Ivoire could easily and safely be shipped to France. That historical encounter accounts for several people who were born in Burkina, ending up as residents and citizens of Côte d'Ivoire.

Sudden Deaths in Today's Ivorian Politics

Alassane Ouattara (commonly called ADO) became president of Côte d'Ivoire in December 2010 when elections were organized, after the civil war that ravaged the country from 2002 to 2011. His respectable track record at the IMF and the Central Bank of West African States and his good reforms as prime minister of Côte d'Ivoire raised hope in many Ivorians and observers. The nerve of that war partly lay in the fact that the southerners who considered themselves as pure-blooded Ivorians (a sad term which always causes bloodshed) realized that most of the wealth of the country was in the hands of Ivorians of Burkinabè descent. Other analysts attribute more complex reasons to that war. Alassane Ouattara could be re-elected only once, and each term was five years. But in 2020, he surprised many people with his decision to run for a third term of office – made after Amadou Gon Coulibaly, his prime minister and hand-picked successor, died in July 2020 when he was said to be recovering after a heart surgery he underwent in France. That caused turmoil; Ivorians were flabbergasted and voiced their opposition to this sudden maneuver.

Then, President Ouattara appointed Ahmed Bakayogo as vice president to replace the late Gon Coulibaly. Ahmed Bakayogo died on March 10th, 2021, in Germany, where he was being treated for an illness. The main question and rumors that are circulating almost everywhere in the sub-region are the following: has Bakayogo been poisoned, as some believe? How could two prime ministers die in so short a time? What does President Ouattara gain by doing that? Is he carrying out a civilian version of what his guest and friend Blaise Compaoré did in Burkina Faso? This is an issue worth following closely. President Alassane Ouattara is surprisingly running for a forth term, something which violates the constitution of the country. Much tension prevails in the country, because of the disapproval that this 4th term issue has raised. The current tensed relations between

Côte d'Ivoire and Burkina Faso (a tension that culminated in the death in Côte d'Ivoire of popular Burkinabè activist Alain Traoré also known as Alino Faso in July 2025) has created a situation where people in both countries are waiting to see where the antagonism will lead to.

President Ouattara is still known to be a puppet of France, and he is not on good terms with the Burkinabè President who rejected democracy and adopted a Progressist Popular Revolution governance system in April 2025, according to Agence d'Information du Burkina(AIB).

THE FUTURE OF THE WORLD DISCUSSED IN AFRICA: EGYPT COP 27

Many readers welcomed with surprise the fact that the COP27, the most important climate change event was hosted by Egypt in November 2022. When Africa has been considered for a long time as a minor player in international forums and meetings, the choice of Egypt makes many people think twice. The previous one was held in 2021 in Glasgow (Scotland), and the 2023 conference will be in Dubai. COP is the "Conference of the Parties". It is the global decision-making body of the UN Framework Convention on Climate Change (UNFCCC). This brings together every year, 198 countries which are United Nations member states, as well as the United Nations General Assembly observers like the State of Palestine and very few others, to discuss progress and explore ways that can lead to better results. On November 6, 2022, this year's conference kicked off and lasted until November 18 in Sharm el-Sheikh, a resort town with sheltered sandy beaches, clear waters, and coral reefs, filled with bars and restaurants. Is Egypt trying to sell its tourist attraction assets alongside being chosen for this important world event? As climate impacts are increasingly widespread, rapid, and intensifying, this year, the world is at a critical juncture to meet the goal of limiting global warming to 1.5 degrees above pre-industrial levels, as committed to in the Paris Agreement. The consideration of the pre-industrial level is certainly an attempt to reiterate the importance of that time and the negative side of modernization. Pre-modern times were good for the environment, and many scholars claim that the way out for the world is to consider the pre-industrial era and its practices. It is therefore not surprising that pre-industrial levels have become the new yardstick. The Conference took into consideration the previous international decision and measures that were aimed at salvaging the environment and counteracting climate change. Some of those agreements are the Kyoto Protocol and the Paris Agreement. In plain terms, the Paris Agreement is a legally binding international treaty on climate change. It was adopted by 196 Parties at COP 21 in Paris, on 12 December 2015, and entered into force on 4 November 2016. On the other hand, the Kyoto Protocol is an international agreement that aimed to manage and reduce carbon dioxide emissions and other greenhouse gases. We may need Environmental Education and Communication here to put some of these technical terms in plain language for the benefit and comprehension by the general readership: Greenhouse Gas Emissions are the emission into the earth's atmosphere of any of various gases, especially carbon dioxide, that contribute to the greenhouse effect. The greenhouse effect is a process that occurs when gases in the Earth's atmosphere trap the Sun's heat. This process makes the Earth much warmer than it would be without an atmosphere. The greenhouse effect is one of the things that makes the Earth a comfortable place to live in; it maintains the planet's temperature at a level suitable for the development of life. The Protocol was adopted at a conference in Kyoto, Japan, in 1997 and became international law on February 16, 2005. Its goal is to limit global warming to well below 2, preferably to 1.5 degrees Celsius, compared to pre-industrial levels. Those two environment-related decisions are central to the COP.

Concretely, this world environment event adopts the following format: world leaders, ministers, and negotiators come together to agree on "how to jointly address climate change and its impacts". Then, Civil Societies, businesses, international organizations, and the media are present, for transparency, and businesses ensure the accountability component. The Conference ensured that the main goals of the body it emanates from are achieved. So panel discussions, round tables, etc. went alongside the main event, and the panels and round tables revolved around themes and topics that form part of the agenda of the Conference. It might help to recall that the Agenda of this "Egypt Chapter" is the following: negotiations on a new goal for climate finance, to succeed the 100 billion from 2026. The negotiations were supposed to be finalized in 2024, but developing countries argued that COP27 should lead to an 'early harvest' – an initial agreement on a set of basic elements in the new goal. The insistence on some key points shows how they are instrumental in this whole business of saving the world from environmental destruction. The following points were driving the Conference: Keep the rise in global average temperature to well below 2 or ideally, 1.5 degrees Celsius; Strengthen the ability to adapt to climate change and build resilience; and align finance flows with 'a pathway towards low greenhouse gas emission and climate-resilient development'.

The COP 27 is important since the world's leading authority on climate change, the International Panel on Climate Change (IPCC) states that the world is now in a "dangerous territory", and as such, every small delay to proportionate action on mitigation and adaptation is a move closer to irredeemable damage to the climate and its ability to meet human needs. Around half of the world's population is highly vulnerable, and they are 15 times more likely to die due to floods, droughts, and storms. The UN Chief, Antonio Guterres, captured the severity of the phenomenon in his speech at the Conference: "the clock is ticking with the planet fast approaching tipping points that can make 'climate chaos" irreversible; we are on a highway to climate hell with our foot on the accelerator". The dilemma remains, "will humanity ever abandon the pursuit of luxury, which is the first producer of toxins that destroy the environment? How many people are ready to put their cars aside and ride in buses or on bicycles? Will the world ever agree that Africa should pay less because it is the smallest polluter, unlike the US and others, who are then supposed to pay more, in the implementation of the polluter pays principle? They approve these environmentally friendly practices, but refuse their implementation since that reduces their comfort. Is COP addressing the real problem(s)?

SETTING THE RECORD STRAIGHT IN WEST AFRICA: THE TERRORISTS ARE NOT JIHADISTS AND THE FULANI ARE NOT TERRORISTS

The period, from 2022 onward is special for the West African countries that are waging the much-talked-about war against terrorism. The insurgency and violent attacks made life unbearable in almost all countries in Sahelian West Africa. What was initially called a jihadist war against national armies has been correctly re-baptized as a cascade of terrorist attacks. That clarification is of crucial importance and in Burkina Faso for instance (one of the hard-hit countries by the terrorists), religious authorities and other opinion leaders found out that it was urgent and necessary to make that difference, and see to it that the population are clear about the difference, since being aware of that difference creates a clear tableau of the situation.

The Burkinabè went to great extremes in order to point out and educate the population about the appellation that fits the attacks that started somewhere in 2015 in the country. TV programs where religious scholars were the hosts, especially Islamist scholars, made it a point to explain to the general population the difference between jihad and terrorism. The key point of this educational initiative was that the attacks that the West African countries are suffering from are terrorist attacks, not the war of Muslims on innocent civilians. The jihad was a practice in the history of Islam that aimed to convert populations to Islam through 'holy wars'. The practice ended centuries ago, and what is going on these days is simply a terrorist act. This education or sensitization program or campaign played a very important role. In the media now and everyday conversation, attacks in Burkina Faso are linked to terrorists, not jihadists.

This education did immense good to the Burkinabè society, but unfortunately, in many West African countries and several nations in the world in general, the misconception and miseducation that equate terrorist acts to jihadism and Islam made innumerable innocent people to be negatively branded and seen them as public enemies. The miseducation led to the victimization and stereotyping of one ethnic group in particular, which is quite large in West and Central Africa: the Fulani ethnic group. They are called the Peul, Fulani, Fulbe, or Fula, depending on the country where they live, and they speak Fulani or Fulfulde. The Peul ethnic group constitutes 7,8% of the Burkinabè population and lives mainly in the northern part of the country.

The same ethnic group is called 'Fulani' in Ghana, and their population is more disparate and apparently smaller. Statistics pose that a recent survey put the population of Fulani in Ghana at 7,300, but based on the reclusive transitory behaviour of most Fulani herders, their number in the country, including the pastoralists, could be higher.

In Senegal, they represent 22% of the population, as in almost all Francophone countries and Nigeria, there is national perfect harmony, cohabitation, and intermarriages between the Peul and all the other groups of the population. In the case of Senegal, one often reads the harmonious cohabitation between the Fulani or Peul and the Wolof, the Lébou, Toucouleurs, Sérères (Serers), Mandingues, and other ethnic groups in the country. The Peul or Fuani are therefore not discriminated against, are respected, and their life is regulated by the same laws that everybody has to abide by. They live in many other West African countries like Guinea, Mauritania, Mali, Gambia, Nigeria, Niger, etc., and Cameroon in Central Africa. They are often lumped together in the same group with the Puular, but there is a slight difference between the Puular and Peul: The Puular are thought to have descended from miscegenation between the Fulani and other tribes.

A few facts characterize the Fulani: They are nomads who live mostly in the Sahel or low rainfall areas, live by rearing cattle, and feed on milk and grains in general. They are experts in preparing so many dishes based on milk: sour milk, fresh milk, warm milk, half fermented milk, and all these varieties of milk are eaten with millet or corn-based food. Therefore, research shows that they have the lowest child mortality rate because their milk-based diet is the ideal one for children. Some of the main occupations and practices of this group led many people in West Africa (as it happens in every area where there is instability and violence) to hurriedly pinpoint the Peul or Fulani as the agents behind the terrorist attacks: they are a nomadic group, isolated from the rest of the population, they sometimes tend to form an enclave because of their sophisticated beauty (because they come from high Nile). They are integrated into society in most cases, except for a few ones and the majorities are Muslims. They represent about half of the Muslim community in Africa.

The unfortunate disparity lies in the fact that the Fulani or Peul are well integrated into society in countries like Burkina Faso, Senegal, Mali, Niger, etc., but in countries like Ghana, the ostracization of the Fulani has led to less pleasant acts like robbery, sexual assault, and much more. All these crimes are committed against the majority of the national population that does not accept the Fulani as part of them. The bellicose relationship is captured succinctly in these lines by some observers. Over the past 20 years, recurrent and violent conflicts between farmers and Fulani pastoralists have persisted in Northern Ghana. These conflicts mainly revolve around access to and utilization of natural resources such as land and water". Some analysts have it that the whole phenomenon can be reduced to this: since the Fulani are already given "a bad name" as the saying goes and are branded as criminals, they therefore go ahead and commit those crimes; humans act out the names, stereotypes and appellations assigned to them in most cases. In countries where they are integrated into society, such disparity-based violence does not exist. Intermarriage exists between them and other ethnic groups, and the Peul or Fulani live happily.

Since the terrorist attacks started, the general opinion wrongly brands that ethnic group as the terrorists. Some of them might really be behind the terrorist acts, like many other ordinary citizens who are jobless, penniless, and needy, but no research shows that this specific ethnic group is behind the attacks. So, as a result, these men, women and children are shunned in most West African countries now because they are perceived as the terrorists and since the majority of them are Muslims as I initially hinted, that coupled with the general preconceived idea that most of religious violence is the prescription of Islam, then the poor Fulani are posed as the epitome of violence. But in reality, the general remark is totally different and reports contend that there is little that connects the Fulani herders to Boko Haram,(or any form of terrorism) besides the fact that the two groups (Boko Haram and Fulani) come from northern Nigeria, are Muslim, and are likely to speak the lingua franca of the north (Hausa). Therefore, the bloody terrorism bedeviling West Africa is not jihadism, and the Fulani are not terrorists. Knowing that contrast, incongruity, and prejudgment can help identify and combat the real enemy and restore peace in West Africa.

COUP D'ÉTAT WITH A DIFFERENCE: THE GABON SCENARIO

No one doubts the occurrence of military takeovers in Africa now. What started in West Africa in 2020 in Mali travelled to Gabon on August 30, after the coup in Niger in early August. The first four coups, which are spoken about most of the time, respectively in Mali, Guinea, Burkina Faso, and Niger, have a common denominator, which is jihadist insecurity, poor practice of democratic governance, increasing poverty, and anti-French sentiments. The coup in Gabon is different, due to several factors that define it and therefore make it special.

Unlike the first four coups de force, the Gabon scenario put an end to a dynasty, that of the Bongo family that ruled the country for nearly 56 years. Their reign started with 32-year-old Albert Bernard Bongo (later known as Alhaji Omar Bongo Ondimba when he converted to Islam), who became president 7 years after the country became "independent". Omar Bongo was then succeeding Léon M'ba, the first president who was elected in 1961 and passed in 1967. Omar Bongo, who had previously served as Léon Mba's vice president, started the "Bongo dynasty" and ruled the country, solely for 42 years until his demise in 2009. He was then succeeded by his son Ali Bongo, who continued the same iron fist pro-France governance style in the oil-rich country in central Africa. Election results were contested several times under the rule of the son, especially by opposition leader Jean Ping in 2016, but nothing tangible happened. Ali Bongo continued his reign as the uncontested president of the country. The dynasty did not bother in any way to improve the living conditions of the overage Gabonese. The wealth of the country remained in the hands of the Bongo family and their close allies; poverty increased among the populace. The country is known to be suffering an enormous wealth gap: A French financial police investigation in 2007 found that the Bongo family owned 39 properties in France, 70 bank accounts, and nine luxury cars worth a total of 1.5 million euros, according to news agency *Reuters*.

It might help to recall that the grip of France over that country is well known and blatant. Gabon is one of the "favorite" backyards of France on the continent. Its strategic location and natural resources led France to develop a special interest in that former colony. The French military presence in Gabon is one of the most robust on the continent. The Swedish Defense Research Institute states that 350 French bases and installations are in the country. Other bases are in Djibouti, Côte d'Ivoire, Senegal, etc. The wealth of the country made it a pole of attraction for many Africans seeking greener pastures within the continent, and the increasing number of migrants caused the adoption of stringent immigration laws, making it difficult for Africans from other countries to travel and work in Gabon. The friendship between Omar Bongo and French presidents like François Mitterrand and Nicholas Sarkozy was overt, and the former used to boast about it. Omar Bongo was, to the astonishment of many Afrocentrists, proud of his closeness to the power in Élysée Palace in Paris, and President Sarkozy referred to him as a "great and loyal ally of France". His son Ali Bongo followed his father's footsteps and did practically nothing to rock the boat: the oligarchy, as some analysts call it, continued, unperturbed. The only little gesture that was not in line with French neocolonialism was noticed when the country joined the Commonwealth in June 2022. Several reasons are attributed to that semblance of shift. Some critics have it that the ousted president, Ali Bongo, had part of his education in the UK, although he did all his studies either in France or French schools in Gabon. It therefore does not come as a surprise when the President, who was deposed on August 30th and placed under house arrest, was seen pleading lamentably and telling the Gabonese people, "I beg you, go on to the streets and make noise". That was his way of inciting an opposition to the coup. Indeed, Ali Bongo is said to have made history as the president with the shortest third term, one of 30 minutes, since he was deposed by the military just 30 minutes after he was proclaimed the winner of the elections.

The coup in Gabon is not a leap out of the French neocolonial arena, while the previous coups have overtly shown such a penchant. The coup in Chad, which is seen by many as a simple replacement of Idriss Déby by his son Mahamat Déby, not a military takeover, is in that respect slightly similar to the Gabon event, except that electoral frauds are cited as one of the main causes behind the coup in Gabon. The commonality between those 2 coups lies in the fact that each of them occurred in a French-speaking country where a military officer took over as president, and no drastic condemnation of the French policy is made. So, the Gabon coup differs from the grassroots revolts that occurred in the first four countries I previously mentioned. Those coups were caused by the discontent with French manipulations that create terrorist insecurity, since many observers pose that the terrorists are simply people handpicked in certain countries, then trained and equipped by France to cause an insecurity that will call for the military assistance of France. Such analysts therefore contend that jihadists are products of the French military, unlike the general opinion that makes them believe that all jihadists are violent Muslims linked to Al Qaeda.

Another factor that makes the Gabon coup different is the background of the coup leader. Unlike most of the first four, the coup leader in Gabon is not a young military officer and newcomer on the political scene. General Brice Oligui Nguema is said to be well-known and unanimously approved by the top military officers of all the defense units in the country. Although he is the chief of the republican presidential guard, just like the coup leader in Niger (General Chani), General Oligui Nguema never showed any anti-French sentiment, and he is seriously close to the dynasty, since he was once the bodyguard of Bongo, the father. He made no declaration whatsoever that goes against the interests of France, and as a result, France and the international community did not condemn this coup as they did in the case of the first four. While heavy sanctions were administered to the military regimes in Mali, Guinea, Burkina Faso, and Niger, no real condemnation was uttered about the Gabon coup. The Economic Community of Central African States (ECCAS) condemned it and called for dialogue to return the country to civilian rule. UN Secretary General Antonio Guterres expressed concern over "reports of serious infringements of fundamental freedoms" during the contested election, but urged all parties to respect the rule of law and human rights; other relatively mild "castigations" emanated from certain organizations. Is it because former President Ali Bongo was no longer useful to France and de facto had to be replaced? That could be a reason, since he suffered a stroke in 2018 and was perceived as incapable of governing efficiently. Others point out the fact that the country joined the Commonwealth, a move away from the Francophonie, the coalition of all former French colonies, a sure apparatus that guarantees the continuation of French neocolonialism.

All these factors point to a semi-palace coup, where the oligarch was simply deposed and replaced by another leader who might not truncate the political French grip over Gabon. The new leader might maintain the pro-France policy, and that could lead to another coup, since he will be seen as a traitor by the overage Gabonese who are suffering under the socio-economic malaise that Francophone Africa in general is currently going through. A second coup that echoes the voice of the downtrodden, the masses, and the repudiation of France, as we observed in the first four countries, is a probability if the government does not follow a clean-cut progressivist path. The new regime pledged to continue public services in the country and to follow the country's commitments domestically and internationally. To many, this therefore looks like a "mild" coup, if that could be said, a simple anti-dynasty move. The coming measures and decisions constitute what really captures the interest of many. Will Gabon join the group of the first four, who are known for their radical, anti-French, trenchant views?

GUINEA: A DIVERGENT JUNTA

Guinea is one of the West African countries that has experienced a coup these recent years. It was the second one, after Mali, where Colonel Goita (now general) toppled in 2020 the government of Ibrahim Boubacar Keita. He found the latter to be manipulated and inefficient. Hopes were high, and proofs of a link between Colonel Mamady Doumbouya's takeover and those in Burkina and Mali were revealed: Populations thought that these three coups were fueled by an anti-terrorist, anti-French (to some extent) sentiment. It was said that secret communications existed between the Guinean president and the leaders of the junta in Mali and the then leader of the Burkina Faso junta, Lieutenant Colonel Damiba, who was toppled a few months later by his brothers-in-arms. The media revealed information that the three army officers took part in several military maneuvers, like "Flintlock" in 2019 in Burkina Faso. Other sources went to the extent of unearthing a continuation of secret exchanges between the 3 military men after these initial encounters.

Prudent observers noticed very early signs of difference or divergence in governance style of Guinea's young and charismatic leader and that of the young and popular military rulers in Mali and Burkina. Many said that Guinea's president, Doumbouya could not adopt a radical progressivist and anti-French attitude like Burkina and Mali, and the reasons behind that resistance and persistence of the ties between Conakry and Paris are the following, among others: Colonel Doumbouya is a French legionnaire, which means that he is a French soldier, to a large extent. I wonder if one can refer to him as a "former French legionnaire" since the recitation of such delicate oaths is complicated. He spent several years living and training as a soldier in France, and on a more personal level, his partner is a female French gendarme, as sources divulged. These and several other factors led many analysts to foresee the impossibility of a total breakaway from the former colonial master. This subtle preservation of ties with France started to disenchant many analysts, who had hopes for the return of a new Pan-African verve as it had occurred in the other two countries. The hesitations or timid gestures that could be interpreted as the persistence of certain neocolonial traits translated into another important decision: When the juntas in Burkina and Mali expressed and manifested their dissatisfaction with ECOWAS that they saw as a manipulated institution at the beck and call of Western nations, a feeling that went further to the extent of Burkina, Mali and Niger (The Niger army orchestrated a coup and joined the camp of anti -Western countries) opting out of the ECOWAS bloc. Guinea did not make any move of that sort. The government made statements like "an attack against Niger is an attack against Burkina Faso, Mali, and Guinea", when military attacks were envisaged by ECOWAS and their Western allies, especially France, against the Niger junta. Other political and socio-economic decisions led to the probable existence of a good relationship between the 4 juntas, but nothing significant was found. Colonel Doumbouya's stance was not what most people expected from him.

Part of the surprise came from the fact that he was not as radical and anti-imperialist as the governments in Burkina, Mali and Niger.

Guinea's "push and pull" attitude became clear when the country allowed Burkina and Mali (Niger will also benefit from that measure) to use the harbor of Guinea for trading purposes. In a total revolt and condemnation of African puppet governments, Burkina and Mali stopped using the Tema harbor in Ghana for some time(it is currently reversed, Tema harbour is now being patronized by the Burkina Faso authorities), a crucial point for their import and export. In a bid to assist the junta that turned into a transitional government, with the solid and massive support of the populations, the proposal made by Guinea would be perceived as a sign of solidarity with the new anti-colonial moves in the other countries. By doing that, Guinea took a step towards the quasi-effacement of the remnants of neocolonialism. That was the maximum Guinea would do in that context marked by the return of nationalism. Unlike the others, Guinea did not leave the ECOWAS bloc and the regime in power in Conakry is not so popular. While in Burkina, and Mali, patriotic policies filtered into all spheres of the nation and national languages were elevated to the "supreme" position that was hitherto occupied by the French language in the national administration and day-to-day activities, Guinea did not attempt that sort. Such a shift was unimaginable there, and the entrenched position of the former colonial master remained.

In the countries where coups occurred, aside from "kicking" French soldiers out was an embrace of relations and ties with Russia and the much-talked-about Wagner militia; in Burkina, particularly, populations bought into the policy brought on board by Captain Traoré, the current president. Some of those policies include a robust anti-terrorist fight. That measure comes with a lot of financial sacrifice that the Burkinabè acquiesced to. Once in a while, someone might be heard saying that much is deducted from their income because of the anti-terrorist "war," but these are far from a general and real disapproval. At least, no mention is made of an insurrection or discontent, or a revolt against the *effort de guerre* now turned into *effort de paix* or support of the anti-terrorist fight, and the return of peace. Almost all commodities purchased by citizens attract a tax that goes into the funds of the anti-terrorist battle. A euphoria of support and general satisfaction prevails in the 3 countries that emphasized the search and exploitation of the numerous massive mineral resources they possess. Coincidentally, these governments are applying to a large extent the policies and leadership of the Burkinabè former president, Thomas Sankara.

None of such an approval and national solidarity emerged in Guinea. The media made mention of a coup attempts against President Doumbouya. An atmosphere that somehow resembled that of the government that Doumbouya toppled in 2021, led by Alpha Condé, is apparently coming back. Although the media, during the first days of Doumbouya's reign recalled some degree of negligence that Doumbouya had for the overage soldiers of the Guinea military (he allegedly underrated or belittled them as ill-trained men among others), no one suspected the current socioeconomic and political situation. The cost of living has reached an unbearable point, and inflation is unprecedented. The price of rice, the most popular food, has increased vertiginously, and freedom of speech is allegedly muffled, electronic communication and media networks are shut down. Sékou Jamal Pendessa, the leader of the union of media workers, was arrested. Protests erupted against the transitional government, and 2 youngsters were shot dead. To top it all, the government was dissolved on February 19, and recent news contend that economist Amadou Oury Bah has just been appointed as prime minister. A general strike brought everything to a halt in the country for days.

Fervent Pan-Africanists and hard-core leftists and anti-colonial observers are seeing their dream being nipped in the bud. Those who were jubilating about the return of the ultra-nationalist, patriotic and leftist ideology and governance of former president Sékou Touré, the revered revolutionary Pan-Africanist are disappointed. The government in Conakry did not reach the anticipated expectations.

REPOSSESSION OF KIDAL AND THE BIRTH OF A NEW UNION

On November 14th 2023, the armed forces of Mali carried out a mission that will remain engraved in memories for years: Kidal, the vast part of the country, close to the border with Algeria is 260 000 km^2 and has a population of 25,617. Kidal is therefore as vast as Burkina Faso as well as Ghana in landmass. The name of the area comes from the main town, which is Kidal, a town that lies 285 km or 177 miles northeast of the country. This area has a special history and represents a multifaceted military and diplomatic discourse and a series of events. It was forcibly cut off from the national territory of Mali for years, and represented the bastion of the rebellion that terrorized that area in West Africa (Burkina, Mali, Niger, etc.).

On 30 March 2012, Kidal and its military base were captured by the National Movement for the Liberation of Azawad as part of the Tuareg rebellion for the independence of Azawad. A spokesman for the Malian military junta justified their loss of that part of their country to secessionists in these words: "To preserve the life of the people of Kidal, the military command decided not to prolong the battle". Two influential cities, with a cultural, economic and strategic location were therefore no longer under the control or administration or governance of the Mali national authorities: Gao and Timbuktu were captured within the next 48 hours, and on 6 April, the National Movement for the Liberation of Azawad declared the independence of Azawad from Mali. It might help to shed light on Azawad itself: It is a movement founded in October 2011 and is mostly made up of the Tuareg ethnic group, a large Berber ethnic group traditionally nomadic pastoralists that principally inhabit a vast area stretching from far southwestern Libya to southern Algeria, Niger, Mali, Burkina Faso, and northern Nigeria. Some of the

Azawad people are believed to have fought in the Libyan army during the 2011 Libyan Civil War, the war that led to the dislocation of the stable and prosperous state of Libya and subsequently set the whole sub-region (part of West Africa and the Sahara area) ablaze since weapons started circulating without any control, after the Libyan war that ended with the assassination of one of the most charismatic and visionary leaders of Africa, Colonel Muammar Qaddafi. The Azawad movement is suspected of having links with Al-Qaeda.

Kidal was in reality not only a geographical space that belonged to the rebellion in Mali, it was also the strategic location of the brains and skills behind the civil secessionist war in the country, and the terrorist attacks in the sub-region. The weapons, camps and all the military logistics of the Tuareg rebellion in Mali were in Kidal. The area was also known to be rich in oil and other precious mineral resources and water bodies that are of crucial importance to the life of that Sahelian country. So the loss of Kidal was a real blow to the nation, and repossessing it was a target that would rejuvenate life in Mali and bring back peace. The UN peacekeeping troops, the French military assistance posed as agents that were working towards the materialization of that wish or dream of a whole nation. But the presence of those foreign troops did not help in any way. The paradox lies in the fact that right after the Malians booted the French military base out and ordered the UN troops to leave, Kidal automatically fell. When the Bamako government asked the UN troops to leave, they simply vanished, leaving no information or details of any type that could be useful to the Malian army. In other words, the French and the UN troops were a buffer force that protected the rebellion in Kidal and undermined any effort of the Malian army geared toward the reconquest of that northern part of the country. Sources claim that the oil, gold and other resources made the area of Kidal prosperous. Jobs were created, and Western countries that were interested in exploiting the resources of Africa were in good business.

When in November 2023 the Malian army and the Wagner mercenaries moved on to Kidal, the bastion could not resist. The Tuareg terrorists who were ruling the area fled since they realized how incapable they were, vis à vis the strength and capacity of their adversaries. Populations could be seen jubilating in the streets in many cities in Mali that day, and for the first time, a Wagner mercenary was seen, without a mask; his face could plainly be seen. In their debacle, the Tuareg warlords of the area claimed that their departure was a tactical retreat, when it was obvious that they had been defeated. The situation was therefore the reign of an anti-West (especially anti-French) and national, patriotic, and liberation political system. Many think that the alliance between Russia and the West African states is as dangerous as the imperialistic presence of the former colonial powers like France, while others refute that hypothesis, claiming that every nation is sovereign and has the right to strike an alliance with whoever they choose to partner with, and add that Russia has no former colony and cannot be as exploitative as capitalist Europe or America. What cannot be denied is that France lost her influence over her former West African colonies (Mali, Burkina, Niger and Guinea we add "to some extent" to the case of Guinea for other reasons) and Russians seem to be the allies of these countries and the partnership with Russia appears way less poisonous than the quasi-occupation of Western states, especially France. Another new dimension in all this is that France fell into a state of weak economy that needs the support and control of the EU, as Greece was some years ago, and the African countries that severed ties with France are making giant steps forward and three of them are formed a union, coming together into the united nations in that part of West Africa. Mali, Burkina Faso, and Niger worked feverishly towards the erection or birth of the Union of Sahelian

States, *Alliance des Etats du Sahel* (AES) in French. The ministers of foreign affairs, then big shots of the economy and certainly military Chiefs of those three countries met several times, while the presidents were consulting and trading ideas. Each of the 3 countries is generally known to be a poor Sahelian former French colony which suffers terrorist attacks.

The current natural resources in those 3 nations are like a miracle: the area in general was said to have no precious resources with no access to the sea. Those conclusions were the results of biased and false "surveys" that ended up with the statement that the 3 countries had no wealth and needed foreign assistance to survive. Analysts contend that those studies were conducted by France, which had inculcated a mentality of the poor in the 3 nations, while waiting for the appropriate time to pillage the resources. The manipulations of Paris have been unveiled and the Union of the Sahelian States is a very confident and well-planned emerging entity that will do the following: make a common currency, an airline company for the easy movement of people and goods, and above all, a harmonious exchange of resources and their ally Guinea will provide a way to the sea, a harbor for maritime trade. That seems less likely of impossible now, since Guinea is distancing itself from the countries of AES. In the AES zone, each area will supply what it has to the union: Burkina Faso grows a lot of cotton, Niger is the first in Uranium reserves, and Mali leads in cattle breeding hence, meat production. This means that each country therefore became like a state and a federal government has the final say, as we see in every successful union.

This bold move is making most Western countries tremble; they worry about the interruption of their siphoning of the wealth of West Africa, and they certainly dread the fact that other African countries might follow suit.

RAMIFICATIONS OF THE NIGER COUP: ECOWAS AND SOCIAL COST OF MILITARY INTERVENTION

When General Abdourahmane Tchani overthrew Mohamed Bazoum on July 26 in Niger, some were surprised since the general had turned against the man whose security he was entrusted with, as the commander of the presidential guard. Others certainly saw in the coup an expansion of the coup fever that got hold of West Africa about 3 years ago, starting from Mali and Guinea.

The Economic Community of West African States (ECOWAS), the West African 15-member state organization, which is chaired by Nigerian president Bola Ahmed Tinubu, threatened to use military action with ECOWAS troops and the support of France in particular and NATO and the EU in general, against the junta if the ousted president, Mohamed Bazoum is not reinstated. That decision sent shock waves across Africa and beyond: Forcing a reinstatement of the ousted president would mean ignoring the needs, wants and aspiration of the people of Niger whose support of the coup is obvious and they were citing the following to justify their position: the quasi-incapacity of the deposed government in managing the economy of the country, the government's failure to ensure security against the terrorist attacks and their contribution to strengthening the grip of France over the country. An ECOWAS-led military action would certainly come as a surprise because of the following reasons: ECOWAS is really a toothless bulldog today, despite what was said by the chairman, President Tinubu of Nigeria. Leaders like Ghanaian President Nana Akufo-Addo disappointed people by their instantaneous condemnation of the coups in West Africa; Alassane

Ouattara of Côte d'Ivoire did not do better, and it is common to hear that ECOWAS executives might be on the payroll of the EU and the US. Countries like Burkina, Guinea, and Mali see such a military intervention as a declaration of war against them and pledged to come to Niger's rescue should any external factor try to meddle in the internal affairs of the people of Niger. Situations of that type weaken ECOWAS, since the institution was gradually losing the trust and support of many of its members.

Liberian former president George Weah earlier said that the West African institution legitimizes certain dictatorships, and condemns others. The first ones are often called "constitutional dictatorships" and refer to the forcefully renewed illegal presidential terms and the rigged elections which are endorsed by some international envoys and observers whose credentials and objectivity are often unreliable. Many Africans believe that some of the former heads of state who are granted the honor to supervise democratic presidential elections have a suspicious integrity. Some of them are former military rulers or civilian presidents who are said to be corruptible. Then, when African nations decide to sort out their own internal disagreements and the national armed forces are allowed to take the forefront in such settlements, organizations like ECOWAS heap suffocating sanctions on those developing countries that are simply practicing the will and rule of the people, in their own way. I wonder if such a practice is not democratic. Secondly, some military officers have their names inscribed in golden letters in annals in Western countries. David Dwight Eisenhower (October 14, 1890 – March 28, 1969) was an American military officer and statesman who served as the 34th president of the United States from 1953 to 1961 and historical evaluations of his presidency place him among the upper tier of American presidents. General de Gaulle (November 1890-November 1970) whom the French see as a leader to emulate was a soldier, whose military skills helped in his political success. It is generally written that he "fought his political battles like a military campaign, using all the devices that he had learned to transform France's postwar international position of weakness into one of strength". Thomas Sankara succeeded, with a coalition of like-minded people in taking Burkina Faso during a period of 4 years, through a progress that 25 years of neocolonial rule (of civilian and military presidents) could not achieve; he was an army officer.

Another worrisome and dramatic turn that a military intervention in Niger could engender is "the north going to war against itself". Niger is historically known as the continuation of Northern Nigeria, the 2 countries have close ethnic ties, and a large number of people live "between" the two countries. The ECOWAS deadline to the junta for the reinstatement of the deposed president produced high anxiety in such border areas, especially in Nigeria. It was already known that the bulk of the ECOWAS troops needed for that military intervention would come from neighboring Nigeria. The Nigerian city of Sokoto which borders Niger is home to the army's 8 Division and anxiety is really increasing. That city sits on a major junction on the road leading to Niger and was likely to be a mustering point for troops before any military action. The complication could be found in the fact that one in every five residents in Sokoto in Nigeria is from Niger or has connections with Niger. Sabon-Gari Girafshi, one of the sprawling suburbs of Sokoto is predominantly inhabited by people from Niger. They feard that a military intervention by

ECOWAS could greatly affect their family members and even jeopardize their own security in Nigeria. A resident who was interviewed by the media expressed his worry because his wife and some of his children are in Niger's capital, Niamey, trapped there because of the coup. Many Nigerians were therefore of the view that the use of force to restore the ousted president in Niger could be catastrophic. "For Ecowas to go to Niger with the intention to take back power from the military to civilians, we don't wish for that, God forbid. It's like erasing our history," one of them said. A 59-year-old woman who hails from the city of Dosso in Niger, but has lived most of her life in Sokoto in Nigeria after getting married to a Nigerian man, fears for her son's safety since he is currently living in Niger.

The hope laid in the fact that although West African military chiefs said they had agreed on a plan for possible military intervention, ECOWAS continued to push for a diplomatic solution. Sanctions were imposed on the coup leaders and borders were closed in Niger. In addition, Nigeria cut electricity supplies to its northern neighbor. Many other border towns in Nigeria were feeling the impact of this tension and Illela, (about 80km or 50 miles) from Sokoto is one of them. It's a commercial hub, but it was then wearing the look of a community under economic stress. Lorries loaded with perishable goods were parked, and drivers could be seen, either sleeping or sitting with their phones or radios, waiting for news of the latest developments about the border. The general opinion in Nigeria was that the option of military intervention should be taken off the table, since such a decision could only come from the Nigerian parliament. Nigeria is so pivotal in this equation because it is the most populated country among the members of ECOWAS and accounts for almost half of ECOWAS's annual GDP; the headquarters of the West African institution is in Abuja, the capital city of Nigeria. Nigerian President Bola Tinubu who also chairs ECOWAS was being criticized in his country for his inclination towards military intervention. Many believe that he was bitter about the coup in Niger because he suffered and had to go into exile during the ruthless military regime of former Nigerian president, General Sani Abacha.

The wait-and-see situation was linked to a socio-economic crisis which is the result of a decision taken by most of the heads of state of ECOWAS, probably backed by the EU and NATO. The rule of democracy is certainly good, but should millions of people suddenly see their living conditions flipped over because a democratically elected president was found wanting and got toppled by the military in his country? Is the new leader in Niger opposed to a transition? ECOWAS could be descending too heavily on Niger and part of Nigeria in general, not only on the junta in power in Niamey.

AFRICANS FIGHTING IN THE RUSSIA-UKRAINE WAR

When Russia invaded Ukraine in February 2022, the major speculations around the war were what were the reasons? How long will it last? But not many thought that it would have a direct and physical (human) repercussion on Africa. Some of the most acute effects that Africa suffered were equally felt all over the world. A vertiginous inflation that swept the whole world touched Africa too. Another main fact that is attributed to Africa is the historic gesture of the former Senegalese President Macky Sall, who "pleaded" with President Putin to open the way for the circulation of grains. While people thought that he was asking for grain that could be consumed by Africans, the reality was that the grains were meant for European countries that heavily rely on the wheat produced in that part of the world. Some patriotic progressive African leaders condemned the former Senegalese Head of State for stooping so low and showing the hegemonic impact of Western countries over several African nations, including Senegal.

A question like "what is in it for Africa" did not seem necessary; no one thought that Africa or Africans would get involved in that war in any way. The only interactions or ties of collaboration between Africa and Russia can be traced to the USSR (the Soviet Union) era, when diplomatic ties existed between Moscow and countries that espoused leftist ideology. The Marxists, Communists, and Socialists opted for ties with the Eastern bloc, as it was called, and the Western bloc, simply was the Western capitalist giants like the US, UK, Germany, etc. China, North Korea, and Cuba were part of the Eastern Bloc before the Non-Aligned Front was put in place. That division "resonated with what was termed as the Cold War, the silent threat and antagonism brewing between the two poles. Each of the poles had their allies all across the world. So, African countries that had cooperation(s), with the Soviet Union stressed the following sectors in general: Training African students and professionals, especially in fields directly related to development (Medicine, Agriculture, industrial work, etc.). Military cooperation existed between Moscow and African countries, where revolutionary, nationalist, and anti-imperialist ideology was at the center of national politics. Certain Southern African countries, like Angola and Mozambique, that were fighting an anti-colonial war against Europeans who clung so tightly to the "colonial booty," sought Soviet military assistance. West African states like Mali, Burkina, and Guinea had both socio-economic and military links with the leader of the Eastern Bloc. Many medical doctors, army officers, and educationists (teachers and University professors) in those African countries were trained in Russia. Although the Soviet Union is now dislocated, exchanges of various types take place between African countries and the former states of the Soviet Union. Ukraine was one of those states.

For months, the general opinion was served with startling news, information that was difficult to predict. The essence of it is that African soldiers are fighting in Russia and Ukraine. Details had it that those young men and women (the large majority are men) from several African countries enlisted on one of the 2 sides of the war front. Headlines like the following were common in the media: "Africans fighting in the Russian-Ukraine war, a Sudanese young man among those fighting for Ukraine," and many others. While

African nations in general have refrained from meddling in the war, individuals decided to get involved for several reasons: the search for higher income, bleak economic prospects at home, seeking greener pastures that often come with new nationalities, and religion-related factors. Some media outlets plainly pose that "The promise of high pay and even Ukrainian citizenship after the war proved tempting for many".

Unfortunately, the socio-political and economic conditions are ripe in Africa for such an adventure. Terrorism has gotten hold of many states to such an extent that the sovereignty of the nation-states and the rule of the national authorities are trampled. A country like Burkina Faso regularly broadcasts statements and partial pictures of former terrorists who were captured by the national army and converted or swore allegiance to the nation, hence proclaiming their patriotism. Such young men are learning new trades in most cases in order to be reinserted into society. It is therefore not a surprise when African youngsters in their 20s or 30s enlist in this war. No reason has been so far unveiled when it comes to the exact recruitment process, but many national authorities are said to have warned their youth not to join that war. These fighters are called "soldiers of fortune", or African mercenaries, and their numbers are about hundreds in the Ukrainian camp and around thousands in Russia.

General information has it that both Russia and Ukraine appealed for support in order to boost their manpower at a certain stage in the war. Both Ukraine and Russia are said to have recruited fighters from Africa and Ukraine, that faced a manpower shortage early in the war, made a global appeal for volunteers. Ukrainian President

Volodymyr Zelenskyy is said, to have appealed in 2022 to "pro-democracy nations" for support, and the outcome was that around 20,000 volunteers worldwide expressed interest in joining the fight. This call to arms apparently resonated with hundreds of Africans from countries like Nigeria, Kenya, Senegal, South Africa, and Algeria. These young Africans were bearing the weight of the dire straits mentioned earlier. But the reality of the war, as usual, is far from that rosy picture painted for potential recruits. News reports of captured or killed African fighters, probably to highlight the dangers involved, paint a really grim picture. One of the reports makes mention of an Angolan Russian soldier, whose parents are Angolan and Russian, and that could be another proof of the Russian presence in Angola a few decades ago.

The impact of the Russian-Ukrainian war on Africa is therefore deep, massive, and complex, a reality that remained unknown for years. One of the main apprehensions that emerge here is a scenario similar to the post-war Libya one. With such a long war and many nationalities and mercenaries involved, weapons easily circulate without control, and that could be a real recipe for disaster, in a geopolitical context which is already bellicose enough.

PART II

THE SOCIO-ECONOMIC DOMAIN

THE NANA BENZ OF TOGO

This name Nana Benz refers to wealthy business women in Togo, a West African country which covers 56,785 km2, with a population of approximately 8 million. The Nana Benz started trading very early in textiles produced in Europe, Asia, or sometimes in Togo, when the foreign textile companies settled there. The Nana Benz have always been a socio-political and economic force to reckon with. These industrious women "metamorphosed" with time, adjusting to the features and requirements of new eras.

How They Started

The word "Nana" is related to "Na," which means mother in many African languages, like Jula and Mina, which is spoken in Togo. In Akan culture in Ghana and Côte d'Ivoire, Nana is the name of a royal in general. In this context, Nana Benz refers to wealthy businesswomen who prospered through the textile trade in Togo. They became so successful that they were riding in Mercedes-Benz vehicles. The genesis of this social class goes back to the 1940s and 50s, before independence, when women traders started importing textile from Ghana and when diplomatic relations between Ghana and Togo went sour over the Togoland issue, those traders changed their business partners. They started dealing with foreign or international textile materials-producing companies implanted in Togo and some of them are: British GB Ollivant, United Africa Company (UAC), John Holt, the French SGGG (Société Générale of the Gulf of Guinea), CFAO (Compagnie Française de l'Afrique Occidentale), and SCOA (Société Commerciale de l'Ouest Africain).

These companies were selling merchandise of many types on the markets along the Gulf of Guinea. So the Nana Benz turned away from their Ghanaian business partners and continued to make money in the textile business with those foreign companies; they made their mark internationally by trading in wax-printed cloth. They were generally women from a modest background who used their determination and skills to become the richest in the country; many of them never went to school, so they could not read or write, but they knew how to trade, and it is generally said with humor that they knew how to count money, which is a fact. They ordered textile materials from Indonesia, and when the commodities reached Togo's shores, the women distributed them throughout West and Central Africa.

The Climax of the Nana Benz Class

The wealthy businesswomen were a socio-economic and political class. They had a refined and strong sense of business. They were dealing only in textiles and were riding in Mercedes-Benz cars. The choice of that brand may be related to the German influence. Togo was a German territory until WWI, when France took over as the colonial master. Not every woman trader could afford that lifestyle. In the 1970s, they rose in prominence and became a cornerstone of the Togolese economy. They gave a famous reputation to Lomé, the capital city of their country, as the West African center for the sale of wax prints manufactured in countries like Holland, Belgium, France, and England. Wax print from Holland is commonly called *"Hollandais"* in French-speaking Africa; it is a prestigious and expensive cloth. Women who wear wrappers or dresses or the general "top and wrapper" made with Wax print in Africa are highly respected. In general, such outfits are worn on special occasions like parties, naming ceremonies, weddings, etc. Research confirms that between 1976 and 1984, 40% of the businesses in Togo were in the informal sector, and the Nana Benz were the ones behind that. They created new dynamics in West African business, and an example is when they established Vlisco as the top-selling textile brand in West Africa. Their influence was among the strongest in African and West African business, precisely. It is therefore not a surprise that they salvaged the national economy during hard times: the budget deficits increased from 13.4% of GDP in 1973 to 39.6% in 1979. Then, in the early 90s, political instability shook Togo, and economic sanctions followed, probably because France was bent on imposing its model of democracy in their former colonies, like Togo. Around the same time, a 50% devaluation of the CFA franc brought other difficult times, economically. These women "owned the country" by controlling the economy, and the government used to hire their Mercedes-Benzes for important guests and state functions. They were a model of women's success and epitomized what most strands of feminism are calling for today. They realized women's emancipation could be achieved through financial control and autonomy. With time, the appellation 'Nana Benz' came to symbolize the freedom, ingenuity, creativity, pride, success, and courage of women. They were appointed to high offices in the women's wing of the ruling political party. A leading Nana Benz, Madame A. Amedome, was appointed Minister of Social Welfare in 1977, even though she could not read or write. A woman did not become a Nana Benz through inheritance or society's choice, but through ingenuity and struggle.

Current Realities: Adaptation and New Gender Paradigm

Today, the Nana Benz have adjusted to the postmodern, fast-growing digital economy and its market. Unlike their mothers or grandmothers, the current crop of Nana Benz study in top-notch universities. That enables them to handle efficiently the business bequeathed to them. Another novel dimension is that the Nana Benz are seen at times as a threat to male domination and machismo. They control the budget in homes, pay the rent, and children's school fees. As a result, many men feel uncomfortable and emasculated in the household. Maybe the new norm is to negotiate with women, with a kind of predisposition based on 'nego-feminism' which means 'no ego' feminism, a strand that contends that men cannot lead a prosperous life without women and vice versa. Reflections and studies on the Nana Benz and Gender would certainly reveal exciting results.

ALGERIA, THE LEGENDARY BETRAYER

France and the Western former colonizers of Africa are losing their influence over most of Africa and West Africa (Burkina, Mali, and Niger) in particular. These three countries took control of their own destiny and severed all important ties with France. That decision came as a result of the realization that almost one century of relations with France was in reality one century of voluntary submission to France, one century devoted to the total surrender of their resources to France, a kind of self-inflicted injury which is difficult to fathom.

From the year 2019 onwards, in West Africa, a fertile ground emerged that would expose the semi-perennial exploitation and siphoning role that France played in West Africa. The development of social media, the young age of the majority of the African population, and the fake democracy that France claimed to have brought to the African continent led to a certain number of coups, and young military officers took over from the "servants" of the Westerners. The pinnacle of these events is the foundation or conception and implementation of the union of three (3) countries in September 2023: Burkina Faso, Mali, and Niger. These countries were referred to as the poorest in Africa and the world; they were identified as nations with no mineral resources, almost no natural resources, and therefore, they had no weight at the geopolitical level.

After these nations moved away from France, several things unraveled: the three decided to rely on their own strength and resources, as well as striking a tight military agreement among themselves. Another fact that appeared with the birth of the Alliance of the Sahel Countries (AES in French) which is now a federation is the strengthening of ties with Russia. All the nations of the AES established co-operations and collaborations of diverse types with Russia, mainly at the socio-economic and military levels. Russian military instructors landed in Niamey and the energy challenge faced by the diverse nations is also being worked on, currently. Atomic energy is what the Sahelian union is working to achieve. In the midst of all this, the hypocrisy of certain countries was also brought to the broad daylight. Of course France was siphoning the resources of her former colonies more than ever, and the UN peacekeeping troops, as well as the French troops that settled in each of those countries were assuring a specific agenda: To defend and secure the interests of France. The Uranium from Niger supplied more than 70% of the electricity in France. The gold and other mineral resources of Burkina served almost the same purpose and the wealth in the underground of Mali equally enriched the Western nations. In November 2023, Kidal, a part of the landmass of Mali, fell under the control of the Mali national army. Observers discovered that this part of Mali, which shared a border with Algeria, was like a country on its own. That rich area of Mali has been controlled by the Tuareg rebellion since 2012. Vast resources of gas and oil were found, and traces of Algerian presence that provided support to Western nations, especially France, abounded. It was therefore obvious that the French troops that posed as buffer units between that rebellious part of Mali and the national Malian authorities were simply safeguarding Kidal so that the terrorists could use it as a safe haven and attack the neighboring countries to create and maintain terror. It also became clear that Kidal entered a kind of secession for the defense of the selfish interests of Algeria and France, among others. When Kidal was repossessed by the Malian army (allegedly with the support of the Russian paramilitary Wagner group), more insight could be obtained from northern Mali and neighboring Algeria. What observers chanced upon was immensely intriguing: Algeria was exploiting and selling the riches of Mali (which are really significant and necessary) to France. The paradox here is broad: France, which poses as the land of Freedom, Equality, and Solidarity, was pillaging the resources of a developing country, through Algeria, a nation that was her ally. Algeria, which was taking pride in her situation as the country that refused French occupation and put up a ferocious fight, unfortunately stooped to the level of a stooge at the service and mercy of France. Algerian gas and oil were unequivocally a product and possession of Mali. Analysts clearly put that France allowed Algeria to rob Mali of her oil and gas since 1962. After such a machination, Mali and other countries in similar situations were branded as "poor with no resources". Sources have it also that the quest for that position as the "conduit for this organized international crime" is what currently encourages Algeria to urge and support Malian terrorists to reconquer the Kidal area, where most of the oil and gas are found. Experts posit that Algeria's supply of oil and gas dropped by 76% since all the pipelines in the Kidal area have been shut down when that area was repossessed by the Malian national army. To make things worse for Algeria, Algeria's bad deeds were exposed when the BRICS said that the oil and gas exploited by Algeria does not belong to Algeria, and subsequently stopped several transactions with Algeria; the BRICS got such information because the Wagner troops were among those who rescued Kidal and those Russians (Wagner members) therefore noticed that the terrorists in the oil-rich Kidal area were wearing Algerian military uniform. Algeria is currently at loggerheads with France because the latter adopted an attitude that seems to privilege another country in the sub-region, Morocco. France even refuses to acknowledge the legitimacy of the Polisario Front, an independence movement opposing Moroccan control of the Western Sahara. To oppose the legitimacy of the Polisario Front means siding with Morocco. So Algeria sees her position as the favorite of France being snatched from her. A historical factor that scares Algeria in this current era is that, almost 50 % of the Algerian territory was made by "chopping off" little land from the following countries: Mali, Libya, Mauritania, Morocco, and Tunisia. The main fear of Algeria, therefore, lies in the fact that with what is happening in Russia and Ukraine, these five countries could easily "re-claim" their borders, in other words, their land mass that was used to constitute Algeria. It is also not a secret that the Kabyle people (an ethnic group from Kabylia, a region of northern Algeria; they are the second largest sub-group of the Berber people, who are Indigenous people of North Africa) are bent on a separation from Algeria. The question asked by several observers now is the following: Since the Alliance (now federation) of the Sahelian countries has the support of Moscow and Beijing (apparently of Morocco also), who will now trust Algeria? How will Algeria survive on less than 80% of her production of oil and gas? How will Algeria continue to pay her debt? This certainly means that the year 2024 might be a tough one for Algeria, whose population must feel serious discomfort. It is therefore normal to wonder how Algeria will explain to her younger generations that, since 1962, she has been robbing the oil and gas of Mali, to benefit her colonial master.

The general overview of Algeria's bright image in Africa's history and that of the world is becoming less and less impressive. Many do not hesitate to state that Algeria has used her position to serve her former colonial master and hurt her neighbor, Mali. The resurgence of new patriotic sentiments in the countries of the Sahel Alliance, an organization to which Mali belongs to, contributes to raising more hope in this context of historic thievery and betrayal on the African soil.

PRECIOUS FOREST RESERVE UNDER THREAT OF EXTINCTION IN GHANA

Environmental protection, global warming and climate change are concepts that occupy a special place in today's global geopolitics. The survival of humanity is directly linked to the state of the environment as it has always been, and that umbilical cord between human existence and the ecosystem has attracted a special attention and concern of late. International conferences are held to sensitize citizens of all walks of like and political leaders as well as industrialists to the rate at which the environment is being violated; forest reserves are decimated at a vertiginous speed by merchants of wood or gold mining multinationals. The Amazon Forest in Brazil used to be cited as the area where this tragedy was unfolding, especially with the ultra-capitalist policy of President Jair Bolsonaro. But today it is obvious that no space on the face of the earth is safe from environmental destruction and its catastrophic aftermath: extreme temperatures, drastic change in weather and rain patterns, flooding, pollution of water bodies, etc. So, what was perceived as the problem of the developed nations or some few developing ones like Brazil is now global. Summits are held and supposedly sacrosanct agreements and decisions were taken or adopted: Rio, Paris, Kyoto and many more. All world leaders pledged to adhere to such lifeline related treaties, except few ones like Trump and Bolsonaro. In 2022 in Ghana, a special area, and national property that impacts the lives of Ghanaians was being jettisoned because of petty politics. Unfathomably, the Achimota Forest Reserve in Accra was being ravaged in broad day light. The Forest Reserve was portioned out to individuals. How could Ghanaians let this happen to them and what do they gain in it? Who are the main people and agents behind that abominable act?

The Splendid Achimota Forest Reserve: A Jewel and Pride of Ghana

It is impossible not to marvel at the features of that part of Accra where the forest reserve covers a strategic location in a popular urban area. Achimota Forest Reserve is located in the region of Greater Accra. The distance from Achimota Forest Reserve to Ghana's capital Accra (Accra) is approximately 7.6 km / 4.7 miles. The trees and plants that cover the area provide breathtaking green foliage as a bird's-eye view, a veritable treasure in environmentalism. Aside from that flamboyant beauty which harbors a life sustaining entity, the reserve has other invaluable traits and functions. It is said to contribute immensely to the continuity of the city of Accra's biodiversity which is necessary for the local economic development, among other virtues. Due to its strategic location, Achimota Forest Reserve provides many environmental sustainability benefits that cannot be overemphasized. Being close to a major urban road that is used by numerous vehicles per day, it mitigates most of the environmental pollutants from emissions emanating from vehicles and can cause significant respiratory problems and other health complications. Other benefits of the precious forest are: air purifier, climate stabilizer (trees and plants regulate atmospheric temperatures), economic significance (timber, tourism, rare animals, food and vegetable); it regulates the cycle of water (checks evaporation and precipitations), medicinal value (trees with pharmaceutical components); it enriches the soil (organic fertilizer through shedding of leaves), and much more. It is the only existing greenbelt in Accra and can be used for training purposes with courses in Biology, Forestry, etc.

The Danger Currently Lurking Around Achimota Forest Reserve

One more time we experience the semi-insane and totally gluttonous role that politics plays in African societies. This forest reserve whose qualities cannot be enumerated and measured, due to their large number is about to disappear, in a nebulous context of Ghanaian politics. Ghanaians were shocked when national media relayed that the Achimota Forest belongs to a family, the Owoo family that are residents in Accra, and whose property must be returned to them. The then President Nana Addo Dankwa Akufo-Addo had just signed an executive instrument declassifying parts of the Achimota Forest as a forest reserve. This is one of the versions that are cited as the beginning of what some term a "lute and share saga", a practice not new in Ghanaian politics. That family is said to be "faceless" since nobody knows who they are and that led many to speculate that the party in power simply intends to develop the forest as a sycophants' private properties and the move itself betrayed the poor environmental policy of the government that pays lip service to the protection of the environment since a Ministry of Environment exists, and a contingent of more than 200 people were sent to a climate -related conference. The question that pops up then is: what prevented the government from buying the forest reserve if it belongs to a family? Above all, Achimota Forest is an Eco- Park, a combination of numerous benefits of tremendous value to the nation.

Another Name at the Center of the Controversy: Kwadwo Owusu Afriyie a.k.a Sir John.

Until his death in 2020, Kwadwo Owusu Afriyie was the Chief Executive Officer of the Forestry Commission and his office was situated at the same forest reserve. He was the Secretary-General of the New Patriotic Party (NPP), then in power. The surprise came to a peak when a will was sighted and confirmed, as that of Sir John. In it, he bequeaths to relatives four parcels of specified and unspecified acres of land in the Achimota Forest and that gave a new dimension to the inexplicable phenomenon. The will contains the following statements: "I give my land situate (d) at the Achimota Forest in the name of Jakaypro Limited and measuring 5.541 acres to the following persons forever: Yaw Amoateng Afriyie, 1 acre, Eva Akua Afriyie, 1 acre. I give my portion of land that I jointly own at the Achimota Forest in the name of DML Limited to Elizabeth Asare Boateng who at the time of making this will is domiciled in the USA forever". The politician went further to disclose that he possesses part of the Ramsar area at Sakumono in the Greater Accra Region, which is a precious wetland that is pivotal in the life of Ghanaians and those in Accra, specifically. Part of this precious national asset is bequeathed to Sir John's relatives: "I give my land situate(d) at the Ramsar area at Sakumono in the Greater Accra Region and measuring 5.07 acres to my sisters Abena Saah and her children, Comfort Amoateng and her children, Abena Konadu and Juliet Akua Arko and her children on equal share basis forever" the will states.

The government says there are no records at the Lands Commission to support claims that the late former Chief Executive Officer of the Forestry Commission, Kwadwo Owusu Afriyie, acquired portions of the Achimota Forest Reserve land. This situation has infuriated many Ghanaians who took to social media, asking explanations for the government that has been under serious criticism for some time now. I find it difficult to imagine how such important national assets like the Achimota Forest Reserve and the Sakumono wetland can be degraded, destroyed, and trivialized in a story of politicians and corruption.

BURKINA FASO AND RUSSIA COOPERATE IN NUCLEAR ENERGY PRODUCTION

The presence of Russia and her influence keep increasing in Africa, especially since the beginning of the war in Ukraine. It is difficult to see in this a maneuver by Moscow in order to turn the world's attention away from the atrocities caused by that conflict since several countries have suddenly called for agreements with Russia. Each of those African countries experienced a coup d'état or series of coups. So, trying to establish a link between the political events in the West African countries and the Russia-Ukraine war is hard. One speculation made by many people revolves around a kind of historical coincidence that led to the "golden age" of Russia in West Africa.

Since 2020, four West African countries have entered or re-entered the context of coups, a phenomenon that apparently was halted for some time, since "Western democracy" was the predominant political approach. Indeed, all African countries, especially the so-called developing ones had literally been forced to embrace or copy the Western governance model. That awkward act led to other flails like corruption, democratic dictatorship since certain elections were visibly rigged but accepted, a military subjugation of Africa to Europe and the US, especially to former colonial powers like Britain, France mostly and Spain and Portugal to a minor extent, probably because of the limited number of colonies those 2 European countries had in Africa. The debacle caused by that blind imposition of the Western political model led some scholars to a call for the assertion and implementation of an African paradigm, a governance system that is endogenous to Africa, an Afromorphous one, and that governance system already exists. Nana Kobina Nketsia V (2013) calls for the Ghana Paradigm. History records that one of the first constitutions in the world was written in the Mali empire in the 13th century. Therefore, democracy and the prosperous transparent political system is not new to Africa. Pre-colonial Africa boasted of a dynamic and admirable governance system.

Some analysts would say that ideologies or political inclinations like capitalism, socialism and communism were all harmoniously concentrated at the heart of the pre-colonial African political machinery. Afrocentric scholars would add that Greece or European nations in general imitated the African political systems, especially that of West Africa in citadels of knowledge and good practices like Timbuktu or Tombouctou in today's Mali. So, what happened around the 1990s in Africa, which is the imposition of foreign leadership model, is the opposite of one of the main political events that occurred centuries ago, when the nations of Aristotle and Socrates learned the art of leadership from West Africa. As every foreign, imposed or hurriedly applied procedure or measure, especially an important and delicate one like political governance, the Western democracies failed Africans, favored Europe and America (to some extent). The game of America in this narrative is mentioned with less emphasis since that country which is rightly called the "New World" did not take part in the colonization process of Africa. It rather designed and practiced an imperialistic system that implanted American hegemony onto Africa, developing nations in the world and the whole world to some extent. The discontent of

Africans with the flails of the "democracies" adopted in the 1990s ultimately led to a cascade of violent military take overs between 2020 and 2023 in Mali, Burkina Faso, Niger, Guinea, Chad and Gabon. The last 3 are problematic since many see them as Western manipulations, while the first 3 are the product of real anger of the masses against one colonial master, France. Trying to find out why all those countries that experienced coups are former French colonies would lead to another lengthy and passionate debate or reflection.

In Burkina Faso, 3 major coups occurred since Blaise Compaoré, the main artisan behind the protection of French interests and the solid control of France over the country was ousted in 2014. The military officers that led those shake ups are Lieutenant Colonels Zida, Damiba and Captain Traoré. The 3rd one is the current president and as it happened in all the other 3 countries where pro-France regimes were toppled, Burkina Faso opted to sever all ties with France and rather strengthen relations with Russia. Mali and Niger. Those countries are said to have adopted that path in the search for a vigorous fight against the terrorist groups and Wagner, the Russian militia is allegedly efficient in that task. Burkina Faso acquired impressive military equipment from Russia in order to defeat the terrorist movements, and also struck other agreements with Moscow in the fields of the military obviously, education, economy; the one that can be called "the talk of the moment" in West Africa is the nuclear energy deal that was signed between Russia and Burkina, right after the Russia-Africa summit in July 2023. The government in power in Ouagadougou took a bold step in an area which is pivotal and sensitive. South Africa is, until now, the only country in Africa that produces commercial nuclear energy.

This agreement between Burkina Faso and Russia will enable the Russian state-owned nuclear company Rosatom to build a nuclear power plant in Burkina, and the country explains that move, with several reasons: Burkina is one of the least electrified countries in the world with roughly 23% of the population having access to electricity. The location of the country at the "heart" of West Africa, an area which is generally deficient in electricity makes it very important for Burkina to be a big producer of electricity that supplies her neighbors. Sadly enough, Burkina has one of highest electricity costs in Africa, according to the former US development agency, USAID. Uranium from Niger, which was being unjustly exploited by France, will contribute immensely in this electricity project. This cooperation will help Burkina achieve one of her main goals: to reach 90% electricity access in urban areas and 50% in rural areas by the year 2030. Burkina Faso currently buys electricity from neighboring countries like Ghana and others, and most of the electricity in the country comes from biofuels like charcoal and wood and oil products account for one third of the energy supply. This agreement requires the training of qualified personnel and according to Burkinabè media, a batch of Burkinabè students and young scholars will be trained in Russia every year in thermal energy "science" and at some point, those ones will train specialists (in the same domain) from Burkina and other countries in the sub-region. The new energy policy has a sub-regional dimension and a Pan-African one as well. Since the signing of the Memorandum of Understanding (MOU) between Burkina and Rosatom, many African nations like Nigeria,

Kenya and Rwanda have decided to build nuclear power plants with the cooperation of Russia or other countries. Most of the military juntas in West Africa are proving to be innovative and visionary.

FIGHT AGAINST CORRUPTION: INTRODUCTION OF E-PAYMENT IN ROAD TRAFFIC VIOLATION IN BURKINA FASO

We are certain that no country can boast of zero corruption in the world. The reality is that certain areas seem to be the haven of that canker, while others have a low prevalence or experience "underground or sophisticated corruption" to preserve or protect their image as examples of good governance or democratic practice. In the US, for instance, financial scandals are not nonexistent. Famous companies and wealthy individuals are involved in gross corruption cases that the media reports on in most cases. A prominent political personality like Donald Trump is currently trying to fight his way out of corruption allegations and scandalous accusations in the US. The general saying in the case of the US is that while decades ago, hard work and self-made people were proud of themselves and their journey in life, they would disclose in public, meticulously, how they made their fortune and climbed up the wealth ladder out of the "world need and want". Money now seems to be the most valued item, particularly for individuals born into wealth. In Europe, we hear of financial, moral, as well as political corruption, and the late Italian Prime Minister Silviano Berlusconi was trapped in this quagmire a couple of times. Corruption is also a reality in Western or developed countries.

Developing countries in general, in Africa, Asia, South America, and Eastern Europe, are labeled as the breeding ground of corruption; their ranking is so low when the corruption index is considered. Increasing restrictions on accountability measures and basic civil freedoms allow corruption to go unchecked. The Middle East and

North Africa remain special cases because their weakness in terms of accountability and fairness lies in the fact that the interests of a powerful few continue to dominate the political and private sphere, and the limitations placed on civil and political freedoms are blocking all significant progress. In Sub-Saharan Africa, armed conflict, violent transitions of power, and increasing terrorist threats, combined with poor enforcement of anti-corruption commitments, rob citizens of their basic rights and services.

Methods or tools (instruments) like Corruption Perceptions Index (CPI), Global Corruption Barometer (GCB)-Africa are frequently used to assess the nefarious practice and these are some of the results they reveal: In 2022, according to CPI, corruption levels were at a worldwide standstill and it might help here to add that what the CPI does exactly is to rank 180 countries and territories around the world by their perceived levels of public sector corruption and the results are given on a scale of 0 (highly corrupt) to 100 (very clean). The first 3 countries were therefore Denmark, Finland, and New Zealand (ranked with 1), and Somalia, Syria, and South Sudan were among the most corrupt, with respectively 178, 178, and 180. This corroborates the general remarks we made above. Global Corruption Barometer (GCB-Africa) concludes in its 10th edition (in 2019) with this note of hope: most people in Africa believe that corruption is on the rise in their country, but the majority remain convinced that as individuals, they can make a difference in the fight against the flail. This barometer also pinpoints the following institutions as the most corrupt in Africa, from the biggest culprit to the smallest: the police, government officials, magistrates/ judges, the office of the president and the prime minister, local government officials, and the least corrupt are NGOs and religious leaders. This tableau certainly presents little differences based on individual countries since this is a continental evaluation. That notion of hope in the fight against corruption, which is echoed by some African citizens, is what is currently materializing in Burkina Faso (West Africa), a country that posed for a long time as a corrupt one, especially during the rule of neocolonial and debatably democratic leaders. Fortunately, this trend is being reversed, and it is said that Burkina Faso is trying to overcome a bad governance and corruption legacy. Bribery and bureaucratic corruption were generally widespread, permeating all sectors of society and affecting the daily lives of the Burkinabè. The extractive industries sector, the judicial system, and the public health sector were seen as the most vulnerable to corruption. A specific example of that anti-corruption policy lies in the recent implementation of the "e-contravention platform", on July 13, 2023, an electronic payment mode of fines by citizens who violate traffic rules and regulations. The measure is the initiative of the current regime in power in Ouagadougou, precisely the Ministry in charge of Governance and National Security, and involves the following: a culprit of road traffic violations pays a determined and fixed amount of money (officially determined and known by the general public) into the accounts of the state, via electronic means. It means that the citizen uses what is generally referred to as "mobile money" or "Orange Money" transfer (the "Orange Money" system is more common in French-speaking West Africa) to pay the penalty into the coffers of the state. No cash is handled by the traffic law enforcement officer (the police in general). Before that, traffic control by law enforcement officials was one of the most corrupt activities: penalties or fines were paid, and the money would find its way into the pockets of individuals. Traffic light violations are one of the frequent contraventions in Burkina, so a fair way of handling the fines collected would provide an amount of money for the national treasury. The measure was adopted to curb corruption in that domain. Many see it to be a salutary move, which contributes to the digitalization of public administration, generates less corruption, helps citizens save time when they have to pay fines for traffic rules violations, and eradicates the phenomenon of "police stations with less available free space" since most of the yard is occupied by a large number of bicycles, motorbikes, and cars seized from traffic rule violators who are yet to pay the penalty. But others are worried by the hindrances that the smooth running of the decision might encounter. First of all, if the fine to be paid by someone who violates traffic regulations is 6,000 CFA (slightly over 10 USD), a road user could negotiate with the police officer and pay her 2,000 CFA, or a third of the legal fine. That would be an agreement between the two persons, and corruption continues. So, pegging the fine with the income of the overage citizen in mind is a sine qua non. So, the "e-contravention" policy coupled with a higher fine might produce the opposite effect, which is more corruption and less money paid into the national coffers. The second apprehension stems from the digital literacy level of the general population in a country where the illiteracy rate is high. Not all citizens use electronic transactions, so they might not be able to make a payment. Other questions are: what shows that the fines that are paid go into the coffers of the state? How ready and willing are police officers when it comes to using the e-contravention device or platform? The electronic network often malfunctions. How can payments be made in such cases? The initial temporary confiscation of the culprits' means of transportation while they make arrangements for the payment of the penalty was to make them uncomfortable for some time. Now that they only have to pay and continue their way, will they be deterred enough? But the general belief is that if Burkina Faso succeeds in making this innovative technique work, it will provide an example that will be emulated by many countries. It is said that more rigorous measures will follow this e-payment innovation.

DID AFRICA GO FULL CIRCLE? FROM THE FREEDOM FIGHTERS' CONFERENCE TO ANTONY BLIKEN'S AFRICAN TOUR

The 1960s were for Africa the years of celebration, of victory for liberation moments, the days of *"indépendance Cha Cha"* in French-speaking Africa. One event that remains engraved in memories is the "Freedom Fighters' Conference" or "All African People's Conference" (AAPC) organized by the first Ghanaian President, Kwame Nkrumah, in 1960. Such a meeting of bold, buoyant, united combatants and strategists who champion the cause of autonomy and self-rule is in sharp contrast with the January 2024 tour of five (5) African countries by the US Secretary of State, Antony Blinken. The AAPC was an assertion of the burning desire of Africans and Blacks in general (since prominent Black Diasporans attended it) to attain freedom by all means, including guerrilla warfare if that is necessary. Why was Blinken then touring selected African countries when in the 1960s, such a phenomenon could not be envisaged because Nkrumah had laid the foundation of a platform that promotes the quest for freedom and liberty, the rejection of parasitic intrusion?

Let us recall the salient features of that congress that brought together black freedom fighters in Accra in 1960.The conference is presented as the brainchild of Nkrumah and his Trinidadian advisor George Padmore, with whom Nkrumah had attended the Manchester pan-African Congress in 1945, when their Pan-African convictions were reinforced. The 1960 conference is the corollary of the "logical" link that the Ghanaian leader posed between the independence of his country and that of all African countries in these words: "The independence of Ghana is meaningless unless it is linked up with the total liberation of the African continent", a statement which was subsequently debated a length and on several occasions but what cannot be denied is that the ideal conviction and motivation behind that statement was then laudable and praiseworthy. It conveyed the urgency, sacrosanct, and pristine features of freedom, liberty, and independence. The December 8, 1960, conference itself is described in the following lines, to be more specific: "Hundreds of delegates from 28 African countries and colonies attended the AAPC. At least 65 national liberation movements were represented. It was the first time many independence movements were meeting each other, networking, and drawing strength and strategy from each other. Tom Mboya, the then-28-year-old maverick trade union organizer who later became Kenya's justice minister and is regarded as one of the East African country's founding fathers, chaired the conference. Martiniquan philosopher Frantz Fanon, who played an active role in the Algerian war of independence from France around the same period, was there — as was Patrice Lumumba, who would later become the first prime minister of the newly independent Democratic Republic of Congo (DRC)". The slogan of the participants was "hands off Africa" and 10 years later, almost the entire continent had declared independence, free from colonial rule, at least at face value. That was the official position of Ghana vis à vis colonialism, since much robust work was done within the country, through a strategy that was not made so much public. The country emphasized ideological training, a treasure that the majority of university graduates from tertiary institutions today woefully lack. That education was provided at the Kwame Nkrumah Ideological Institute in Winneba, which was a compulsory passage for all Ghanaian youngsters before they could enter university, and many political leaders of today's Ghana attended that course. A lot of praise is mentioned about the institution and its program. Aside from that dimension, ideological "baptism" was extended to many non-Ghanaians to assure and pursue the anti-colonial battle. Many leaders of African freedom movements who had been invited by Nkrumah into Ghana were provided with academic and adequate political and military training before they returned to their countries and took up arms. Robert Mugabe of Zimbabwe, Sam Nujoma (the first president of Namibia) are the names mentioned in most discussions. Of course, that defiant penchant adopted by newly independent Ghana was not approved by Western powers, who saw in it a real threat and worked to undermine it. Many kinds of sabotage were carried out after the 1960 conference and all the initiatives that followed it, and some of the Western attacks to that anti-colonial struggle were: the close monitoring of those who were present at the conference, travel restrictions for many of them, and the biggest blow was administered in 1966, when U.S. President Lyndon B. Johnson backed a coup by a group of Ghanaian army officers against Nkrumah while he was away from the country. It is said today that the Pan-African movement fell apart, bit by bit, but consistently, and unfortunately, Africa is in economic chains. The independence that was obtained was followed by a huge disillusionment when African leaders proved to be more harmful than the colonial masters. That led to the eras of the coups d'état, which were followed by the IMF and its stifling Structural Adjustment Programs, SAPs. I am referring to a full circle here since it is possible to capture the trajectory of Africa this way:

the days of hope, glory, bravery, and anti-colonial fight. Then the failure of African leaders guaranteed by the machinations of the neocolonial apparatus, the decline of the national economies, and the ignition of conflicts exacerbated by frustration, anger, and confusion, and the stage of postmodern colonization that we are now living in. The soft power of China, Russia, and the USA is re-creating a scramble over Africa, and the 1884 Berlin Conference is born again like a phoenix. The more recent indicator of that sad state of events is the recent tour of the US Secretary of State Antony Blinken in 2024. There is no doubt that China is imposing itself as a political, military, and cultural superpower. Russia's influence is more overt in certain West African countries like Mali (Burkina Faso and Guinea are said to have, at some point,contemplated hiring Russian mercenaries, but they were dissuaded by the grip of France). Diplomatically, this competition over the soul and bounties of Africa is this: the tour of the Russian Minister of Foreign Affairs Sergei Lavrov in Africa (Egypt, Republic of Congo, Uganda and Ethiopia) from July 24 to 27, while his country is shelling Ukraine; On July 25, President Macron of France was in Cameroon, on a visit that would take him later to Benin and Guinea Bissau. The third voyage of this type is that of the USA diplomat to South Africa, DRC, and Rwanda, a tour that started on August 7, 2022. The hopes and dreams of the Freedom Fighters' Conference or AACP were squashed, and that explains why and how Africa re-entered the inferno of subjugation. From colonization, Africa achieved "independence" and re-entered subjugation. The colonial masters and their brute force and African auxiliaries are now replaced by a more vociferous strangulation that camouflages as political, economic, and other kinds of alliances or cooperation. One would not be wrong in saying that Africa has gone full circle, sadly enough. But this does not mean that the anti-imperialist struggle must be abandoned; it simply means that new tactics are required. The exploiter has adopted a new modus operandi, so the valiant sons and daughters of Africa need to design new strategies to counter the canker.

FRENCH FALLACIES SHAPE CONSIDERABLY CONTEMPORARY SCHOLARSHIP

Each society is making efforts to produce its own image in bright colors. Pre-colonial societies were not so much involved in that competition that reached ferocious levels at some point. Before Western countries created hybridization through their presence in Africa, Asia, the Americas, the Caribbean, etc., one could find on those lands societies that were living with a considerable level of composure, tranquility, laced with peaceful co-existence and harmonious existence with their surroundings. A few examples would be the native American societies or Red Indians before Europeans waged war against them to marginalize them, take their lands away, and force them into the confines of History. In Africa, many communities that are bearing the brunt of the environmental crisis are now hammering the notion of Indigenous Traditional Knowledge (ITK) that is simply a set of rules put in place for the preservation of the environment without residents feeling subjected to any force, or deprived of any favorite activity or consumption. Communalism was also one of the core values of those societies. The relentless drive behind one's own property was almost nonexistent. In a nutshell, pre-colonial societies functioned and relied on these rules with such ease and very little bellicose tendencies. The conquest of territories was a reality, but the peaceful inclination behind such acts cannot be compared to the gluttonous and ferocious urge that guides confrontations and wars in this postmodern society. It is therefore not a surprise when many scholars say that Europe invented the "non-European territories and people(s)". Hegemonic Western nations pillaged the material, cultural, and intellectual resources, wealth, and property of the nations that were prospering in their own cultures and civilizations. Scientific sources record that in order to "cripple" the African, Asian, and American societies that they encountered and admired because of their sophisticated levels of advancement (progress) and self-organization, transmission of knowledge, etc., the West had to brand them as barbaric, backward, savage, and non-developed. That is the essence of the rapport that was posed between Greece and Africa, to mention just one example. Cheick Anta Diop, Theophile Obenga, Joseph Ki-Zerbo, and many who are often referred to as 'Afrocentric' or 'Africentric' or other less implicating terms demonstrated how that process took place. How Western 'elites' acquired knowledge from Africa and committed a double crime: stating the lie that they produced that knowledge which ultimately trickled down onto Africa, and in other cases, the repositories of world scholarship that were situated in Africa were emptied of their content or burned down, once Europeans knew that this knowledge was safely in their possession.

Literacy and socio-political advantage or domination are very important in such contexts, and education is key to the existence and evolution of a society. Hegemonic Europeans created an African whom they called inferior, and that belief had to remain for the existence of those entirely "different" entities. So, children were taught what society wanted them to know and to believe. The inferiority of certain races compared to others was presented as an irrefutable truth that every European child, as well as black children who attended Western schools, had to know. I will also mention only one instance here, which speaks volumes. In French culture and

French literacy, La Fontaine (whose full name is Jean de la Fontaine) is known to be the artist behind hundreds of fables that are used as efficient literary pieces to teach reading, speaking, teaching French culture, and certainly, writing. The beauty of scholarship or intellectual property is its dynamic trait or feature. Several poles of 'interrogation or questioning' have opened on many points of the formally so-called backward nations or "periphery". South America and Africa are some of those zones where European hegemony is being scrutinized and more and more inconsistencies are found in it. Captain John Smith and his rescue by Princess Pocahontas in the Americas proved to be false when the same Captain later wrote that a Turkish damsel saved his life when he was to be put to death, and his life was saved because he was Caucasian, the main feature of 'handsomeness' in the European imperialistic worldview. In the same vein, Africa boasts of prolific research centers like *Afrique Résurrection* (AR), a pan-African media for the new generation, founded by the young revolutionary anti-capitalist and unbowed young French man of African descent, Kemi SEBA. Investigations and research conducted by that center unearthed that the icon that the French are so proud of, because the whole French language and culture stand on it, "The Fables of La Fontaine," does not have a French origin, but rather an African one. Aesop is the man at the center of the discussion; he was known to be a black man, an African from Sudan who was dark skinned, with thick lips, dark hair, a flat nose, and all the attributes of the Black African. *Afrique Résurrection* portrays him exactly this way: Aesop is "620–564 BCE; formerly rendered as Æsop, he was a Greek fabulist and storyteller credited with a number of fables now collectively known as Aesop's Fables. Although his existence remains unclear and no writings by him survive, numerous tales credited to him were gathered across the centuries and in many languages in a storytelling tradition that continues to this day. Many of the tales associated with him are characterized by anthropomorphic animal characters . Aristotle and Herodotus state that "Aesop was a slave in Samos; that his slave masters were first a man named Xanthus, and then a man named Iadmon; that he must eventually have been freed, since he argued as an advocate for a wealthy Samian; and that he met his end in the city of Delphi. Plutarch'. Both camps intersect on one point: Aesop was a black, captured as a slave, found himself in Greece, and introduced an art or genre that was new there: the fables. That earned him a reputation; he is freed for his intelligence, and people come to listen to him. Herodotus calls Aesop a "writer of fables," and Aristophanes speaks of "reading" Aesop and which reveals the scholarship that this black man produced. *Mes étoiles noires* [My Black Stars] (2009) by Lilian Thuram sheds more light on his African origin. On the other hand, Jean de la Fontaine was born in the 17th century (in 1621) and revered as 'one of the most famous and popular writers of his time and is best known for his work *Fables Choisies'*. No mention is made of any inspiration of La Fontaine by Aesop. What we often stumble upon are comparisons that reveal similarities between the fables of La Fontaine and those of Aesop. Here are pieces of such a comparison:

'The Hen That Laid her Eggs of Gold' by **Jean de La Fontaine**

Wanting it all will lose it all /and avarice does that. So let me call /to give some evidence for what I say /on him who owned a chicken who would lay/ (or so in fable we are told)/a golden egg each day.

/Deciding that inside her she must hold/a treasure-house of gold /he killed her, opened her, and found the same/as in the hens from which no riches came.

'The Man and the Golden Eggs' by Aesop

A man had a hen that laid a golden egg for him each and every day. The man was not satisfied with this daily profit, and instead, he foolishly grasped for more. Expecting to find a treasure inside, the man slaughtered the hen. When he found that the hen did not have a treasure inside her after all, he remarked to himself, "While chasing after hopes of a treasure, I lost the profit I held in my hands!"

It would be very profitable to deepen such research and try to find out if inspiration or influences of any type existed between Aesop and Jean de La Fontaine, but such research is scanty and not encouraged, almost non-existent since it is generally believed (unfortunately) that nothing good comes from Africa, from Blacks. So, a French fabulist could not have been inspired by a black person or someone of black descent.

QUEEN ELIZABETH II AND AFRICA

On September 8[th,] 2022, Queen Elizabeth II of England died at age 96. She was born on April 21[st,] 1926, in London to the Duke and Duchess of York (later King George VI and Queen Elizabeth). Had she lived up to May 27, 2024, she would have made history as the longest monarch in world history, thus overtaking Louis XIV of France. She is nonetheless the longest-reigning monarch in British history. Her life has spun several important events in the world: World War II, the end of the British Empire, 14 British Prime Ministers, political and technological changes, and many upheavals in the royal family. A glance at the life of the late Queen unveils a normal and multifaceted life.

She was described as being reserved, shy, with a formal royal side, traits that her mother possessed. Winston Churchill is remembered to have said this about her when she was 2 years old: "The princess has an air of authority and reflectiveness, astonishing in an infant." Her cousins described her as a jolly but fundamentally sensible and well-behaved little girl. Elizabeth was said to resemble her paternal grandmother, Queen Mary, in appearance and temperament. Her younger sister Margaret (4 years younger) was seen to have inherited their mother's devotion, winning charm, and spontaneity. In 1939, the royal family of 4 visited the naval College at Dartmouth, where an 18-year-old cadet, Prince Philip of Greece and Denmark, was assigned to escort 13-year-old Elizabeth and her younger sister during the tour. Elizabeth was smitten, and she and Philip began exchanging letters. Since her parents did not have a son, at age 10, it was known that Elizabeth would someday be the Queen. Her leadership skills became obvious when at age 14 she addressed children during the war in a radio broadcast message during BBC children's hour, when she encouraged children to be brave during air raids and evacuations of their homes and before that, she and her sister had raised money for the Queen's war fund to provide warm garments for the troops during the war. At age 19, she became a driver and mechanic for the Women's Auxiliary Territorial Service, the women's branch of the British military. In 1947, after the war, Philip, a decorated war veteran, and Elizabeth were married. That is when Princess Elizabeth's first encounter with Africa occurred: Just after her marriage to Philip, her parents took her on a state visit to South Africa, where they tried to promote unity between black and white people, and Elizabeth seized that occasion to assert her commitment and loyalty to the service of her people. That tour was a failure since a year later, the Nationalist Party took power and established Apartheid or segregated life in South Africa. That coincided with another important change in the dynamics between Princess Elizabeth's country and her colonies, and many of them were in Africa. Many territories of the British Empire started to demand independence, and then Elizabeth's father, King George VI, relinquished his title as Emperor and King and became the Head of the Commonwealth. In 1952, Princess Elizabeth and her husband, Prince Philip, embarked on a tour to the Commonwealth because King George was too frail for that journey. The couple was in Kenya when Elizabeth was informed of her father's demise; then, following the coronation, Queen Elizabeth and Philip embarked on a seven-month tour of the Commonwealth. Queen Elizabeth became the face of the Commonwealth around the world. The Commonwealth of Nations itself is a "political association" of former British colonies and the UK itself. Although she was discouraged when she decided to visit Ghana (a member of the Commonwealth) in 1961 because of the assassination attempts that targeted Kwame Nkrumah, Queen Elizabeth travelled to Ghana and tried to "win" the country and convince Nkrumah not to side with the Soviet Union since she did not want the Soviet Union to gain a hold over Africa.

The Commonwealth of Nations itself is certainly the strongest tie between the British monarchy and Africa. Since its creation in December 1931, this association of 54 countries, including the UK, is mainly made up of formerly British colonies. Its first members were: the United Kingdom, Canada, Australia, New Zealand, South Africa, and the Irish Free State. The Commonwealth is said to work towards "shared goals of prosperity, democracy and peace". This is certainly a nebulous description. The Commonwealth is more of a way for Britain to keep a hold over its colonies that have fought and snatched independence in most cases, especially in Africa and Asia. The Commonwealth is to the United Kingdom what the Francophonie is to France: a powerful apparatus that ensures hegemonic control over former colonies, whose natural and human resources the former colonial masters still covet. 16 African countries were members of the association up to a certain point, but that dynamics has changed now, since some non-English speaking countries have joined the association. They are Rwanda, Gabon, and Togo (which was previously francophone), and Mozambique, which is a former Portuguese colony. The question remains: have these countries discovered more exploitative and retarding mechanisms in the French, Belgian (Rwanda experienced the rule or influence of the 2 countries), and Portuguese legacy?

Queen Elizabeth II's grandson, Prince William, married Kate Middleton, and Prince Harry married Meghan Markle, an African American actress, and the last couple decided to step down as Senior Members of the Royal family. Harry and his wife gave an "explosive interview to Oprah Winfrey, in which they raised cases of racist treatment and other unpleasant experiences that Meghan received from members of the Royal family.

Research shows that Meghan Markle is not the first black person to enter the British monarchy. Queen Elizabeth II herself is said to be of African descent through Queen Charlotte, the wife of King George III. In 1999, *The London Sunday Times* published an article with the headline "Revealed: The Queen's Black Ancestors". The article states that "The royal family has hidden credentials that make its members appropriate leaders of Britain's multicultural society. It has black and mixed-race royal ancestors who have never been publicly acknowledged". Genealogists have established that Queen Charlotte (who was initially Princess Sophia Charlotte of Mecklenburg-Strelitz from Germany and arrived in 1761 in London), the wife of King George III (1738-1820), was directly descended from the illegitimate son of an African mistress in the Portuguese royal house. Then Charlotte passed on her mixed-race heritage to her granddaughter, Queen Victoria, and to Britain's monarch, who just passed, Queen Elizabeth II. Queen Victoria was Queen Elizabeth II's great-great-grandmother. Historians posit that Charlotte was directly descended from a black branch of the Portuguese royal family: Alfonso III and his concubine, Ouruana, a black Moor.

The past immediate monarch of the United Kingdom, Queen Elizabeth II, who is to be succeeded by her son Charles, the Prince of Wales, shows through her life, work, and lineage the often hidden but important ties that this monarchy has had with Africa, since historical times.

POST COVID AFRICA AND ASIA: THE CASE OF INDIA AND GHANA

Almost two years after the World Health Organization declared COVID-19 a pandemic, the world is coming to terms with the disruptions caused by the virus. It might therefore make sense to take a look at the situation prevailing in some areas that have been hard hit. Despite all the gloom and doom that came with COVID, the pandemic is undeniably an opportunity for world leaders in general to think outside the box and craft novel responses that were previously impossible. It also taught populations how inefficient their political leaders can be in times of crisis, and COVID-19 created a new world order, where only bold, innovative, and problem-solving measures are needed.

The Case of India

It would not be an exaggeration to say that the pandemic brought the world to a colossal economic and financial crisis, which is likely to have long-term structural repercussions. It has laid bare the fragilities of the global economic and geopolitical order. A careful observation shows that the pandemic came to complete a process that had already started; power equations had already started to change, and the power center of the global economy began to shift to Asia, and the new power of certain economies had to be reckoned with: China and India were playing pivotal roles in world economy and geopolitics. India is one of those countries where the first world and the third world co-exist; the richest and the poorest live in the same country. India's handling of the COVID-19 pandemic shares striking similarities with that of several African countries, like Ghana.

Failures

Much criticism was raised regarding the way India reacted to the COVID-19 pandemic. Although the authorities told the world that they were doing their best to contain the disease, some incompetence and ill-intentioned gestures were noticed. COVID protocols were trampled over, and political intentions were paramount. Many contend that at the center of India's crisis is Prime Minister Narendra Modi. First of all, he put in place a Covid-19 task force that, incredibly enough, did not meet for months, and his health minister gave false assurance to the public when he declared that India had reached the pandemic's "endgame" when the crisis was still ravaging populations. Secondly, as infections rose, Mr. Modi allowed large gatherings to help his governing party and burnish its nationalist credentials. Then his government approved a Hindu festival with millions of worshipers, which is another "super spreader" move. To crown it all, the Indian leader campaigned in state elections without a mask at rallies of thousands of maskless supporters. Those are not mean comments but rather, genuine observations made by concerned citizens. Mr. Modi did not exhibit good leadership skills during the pandemic, and that certainly contributed (probably with other factors) to the following pitiful scenes: overwhelmed by new cases, Indian hospitals could not cope with the demand, and patients in many cities were abandoned to die; a shortage of oxygen and hospital beds left patients scrambling. At a tiny crematorium in a Delhi suburb, where seven funeral pyres were still burning, someone conveyed the despair of the nation in these words: "I have lived here all my life and I pass through this area twice a day. I have never seen so many bodies burning together." There were certainly frontliners (in this combat against the pandemic) who must be congratulated, but there are so many others who created havoc through the "black marketing and other things, people who were creating the crisis" as someone said, before adding: "corona itself is not a crisis. They are making it a crisis".

Lessons and Innovations

Rays of recovery are beginning to emerge in India, at many levels: economic, social, and political. The International Monetary Fund (IMF) forecast 9.5% growth in the Indian economy, now that COVID has subsided. At the same time, the world is seeing exponential growth in digital services and infrastructure, from the adoption of large-scale work-from-home arrangements to the use of cloud services and videoconferencing. Many tech leaders have noted that the advancements in digital transformation that were achieved within a couple of months would have normally taken two to three years. These are hopeful signs, but there is still much work to be done.

The Ghanaian Situation

A look at post-COVID Ghana leads to one general remark, very often voiced by many citizens: "The State made money out of the pandemic; the government and its faithfuls made money for themselves." This is certainly disheartening, but reasons and explanations support it. At the onset of the pandemic, the Ghanaian government posed laudable, responsible, and action-driven gestures: water bills were drastically subsidized to the stage of almost "free water". The same applied to electricity, and certain parts in the country were (according to some sources) regularly supplied free hot food. Those actions were justified by the fact that Ghana had received assistance, precisely funds and vaccines, from the US government and the World Health Organization (WHO). The "Covid Fund" was therefore set up, managed by the Ministry of Finance and the Ministry of Health. But now, Ghanaians are almost convinced that they are paying for those utilities and other forms of assistance that were made accessible to them, free. The cost of water and electricity is now extremely high, and it keeps increasing. Credible sources state that just recently, Ghana Water Company and the Electricity Company of Ghana submitted to the government a proposal for new costs or prices that represent an augmentation of 135% if approved, and for these 2 institutions to function properly, extra funds are needed. The question that needs to be answered is "why are extra-funds needed? What was the Covid Fund used for?" These questions are based on the fact the exact amount of cash received as COVID Fund was never disclosed to the public, and another incongruity is the fact that Ghana government claims to have purchased some vaccine, and that was not needed, since adequate quantities were donated to Ghana. The mandatory $50 COVID test for passengers departing from or arriving in the country, at the airport in Accra, certainly yielded a large sum, and the public seems to know nothing about the final destination of the cash. The situation seems to be the same across sub-Saharan Africa: the pandemic was poorly handled in general, and it also became a business venture.

Lessons and Innovations

COVID-19 contributed to familiarizing the Ghanaian public with one of their most basic rights, which is to ask for accountability from their leaders, and veiled corruption was detected. The outcome of the request of the Ghanaian masses is yet to be known, but what cannot be ignored is that the people cannot be taken for granted anymore. Technology took a giant leap, and it is used in all sectors now, from education to healthcare and conferences or meetings. Just like in India, this technological development would have taken a much longer time to be achieved.

FRANÇAFRIQUE, THE APPARATUS THAT SUSTAINED FRENCH IMPERIALISM IN AFRICA

Françafrique is generally known to be the means through which France maintains its sovereignty and control over its former colonies and those of Belgium. In other words, it is France's sphere of influence in sub-Saharan Africa, or France's *pré-carré* (backyard). The term was initially France-Afrique, coined in 1955 by Félix Houphouët Boigny, the first president of Côte d'Ivoire, referring to the close ties between his country and France. That was the beginning of Africa's self-subjugation to the hegemony of France. With time, some critics unveiled the imperialistic ambitions and maneuvers behind the term, and rebranded it as "Françafrique". The French economist and political scientist François-Xavier Verschave is the brain behind that 1998 movement that criticized the alleged corrupt and clandestine activities of various Franco-African political, economic, and military networks, affiliated with Françafrique. When most African countries gained independence around 1959, France still maintained its grip over its former colonies in order to preserve what was the vision of the then President Charles de Gaulle as a global power (or *grandeur*) and as a bulwark to British and American influence in a post-colonial world. The US also encouraged the existence of this neo-colonial "instrument," which to them was very efficient in countering the influence of the Soviet Union in part of Africa. After the Cold War, the Françafrique weakened, partly due to the death of the main proponents of that neo-colonial policy (French businessmen and politicians like Jacques Foccart, Charles Pasqua, and former President François   Mitterrand) and also because France joined the European Union. The multiple coups d'état in Africa and the economic crisis in those countries also contributed to making them less attractive in the eyes of France.

One thing which is of vital importance in the discussion around Françafrique is the leeway it gave to France, in her mission, which was to strategically and completely make it impossible for Francophone Africa to flourish (at any level). Through the channel of Françafrique, the Paris governments put in place the following measures, which are generally lumped together under the general concept of neocolonialism. France adopted exactly 11 measures, which were called "agreements", adhered to by African governments in one way or another, except certain "revolutionary" and military regimes, which opposed some of those measures. But they were too robust to be dismantled by a single country or a single leader. These days, Africa is amazed, and many African countries are envious of the Herculean blow that the military regime of General Assimi GOITA in power in Mali administered to the most dangerous remnants of Françafrique. The critical 8 out of 11 agreements (signed between Mali and France in 1959) that were meant to keep Francophone Africa in general in abject poverty and perpetual political instability were abrogated under the GOITA rule in Mali. After Francophone countries became independent, 14 of them signed those 11 agreements, which are the following, if one attempts to summarize their essence, and by Africa in this list of agreements, I mean Francophone Africa: the "colonial debt" must be invented in order to make Africans pay for the benefits that colonization brought to them; The whole finance of the African francophone countries is confiscated by France; all mineral and other natural resources of Africa belong to France, unless she refuses to take possession of those resources; French construction companies are given priority in the edification of structures in Africa; Military equipment can be acquired (purchased) from France only and army officers are trained by French instructors only; France has the right to send troops and intervene militarily in Africa in order to protect French interests; French must be the official language and the language of education in Francophone Africa; a balance sheet of the finances of the African countries must be sent annually to France. Any country that fails to do so will be forced into a financial crisis; no military collaboration can be signed with any other country apart from France, except in cases when France allows that; the obligation to ally themselves with France in times of war or international crisis. The eleven agreements (they should rather be referred to as "so called agreements" or "real diktats") are still practiced or applied in the fourteen sub-Saharan Francophone African countries and no mention is made of them, even those who tag themselves as specialists on Africa never say a word about this obtuse domination and obvious effort of annihilation. These eleven decisions are what attracted the wrath of France onto Mali, since the 2021 coup d'état (after that of 2020) that brought Colonel Assimi Goita to power; he was later promoted to the rank of General. That second coup is a national historic event that unleashed new choices like the emergence of a strong alliance and military co-operation between France and Russia. It might help to remind readers of the fact that this total alliance with Russia was arrived at, after the civilian government of transition in Mali led by President Bah N'daw realized that the military members of that government (the then Vice President Colonel Goita and his allies) were working towards a rapprochement with Russia and leaked that information to France.

President Macron then ordered the civilian transitional government to put in place a new government, with no military members or ministers. That led to the second coup d'état in Mali (led by Goita), and the rupture that ensued in the relations between Bamako and Paris. Burkina Faso ended almost all forms of cooperation with the former colonial master since the September 2022 coup d'état, and Guinea did not seem to be in the good books of France for some time, but that remark ultimately proved to be false. Steps were taken toward a federation of three former French colonies, Burkina Faso, Mali and Niger and the buzzword for the conscientious youth in Africa in general was "the end of collaboration with former colonial powers, right now." The slogan on their lips in Burkina was "Homeland or death, we shall overcome!". Did that send shock waves to the leaders of the remaining eleven countries of the deceased or moribund Françafrique? Young military officers were being closely monitored in those remaining 11 countries, so that the influence of the three young military presidents of Mali, Guinea (whose leader was initially perceived as anti-French), and Burkina does not extrapolate to those remaining countries of Françafrique, where economic prosperity, peace, and security did not exist, to speak frankly.

GHANA NATIONAL SECURITY SERVICE HEAD OVER EARS IN ILLEGAL MINING

The Ghana law enforcement services or forces were abundantly talked about in 2023, not for good deeds, unfortunately. These institutions have been critiqued over the years for several practices: blatant violation of human rights, open legendary bribery, racketeering, incompetence, etc. Illegal mining or *galamsey*, as it is called in Ghana (we will use that term in the rest of this piece), unleashed so many tongues, for the environmental destruction it causes, the corruption that comes with it, the violence, diseases, loose morals, and so many negative consequences. What was disappointing to the overage Ghanaian is that individuals, dressed in military or police uniform, armed with sophisticated guns, were caught practicing illegal mining. Most of the time, they pretended to be on a mission to arrest illegal miners, when their real interest was to get their share of the bounty emanating from this crime, which had been eating so deeply into the fabric of the Ghanaian society for years. If the national security officers were corrupt enough to descend to the level of such crimes, one wonders where Ghana was heading. Others lamented that they were living in a failed state, many accused the government of its laissez-faire attitude, but what cannot be denied is that a phenomenon which was growing wider and wider in Ghana is the security services, or forces, or national security operatives, indulging in crimes. Who will arrest bandits and criminals who haunt the daily life of citizens? How fair is it when a poor young man who, out of hunger grabs a bunch of plantain and bolts away, or steals a goat to sell it for some little money to buy food, languishes in jail, while the hardened criminals in national security uniform or apparatus of all sorts keep parading or better still patrolling on the streets of the cities, free and intimidating people? The rot was reaching gargantuan proportions and kept aggrandizing, unabated.

A little bit on the genesis of the phenomenon takes us back to the Atewa Forest in the Eastern Region of Ghana, a forest reserve that used to be one of the natural jewels of the nation. Some sources have it that the award-winning movie *Beasts of No Nation* (2015) was shot in that forest. In May 2021, 19 national security officers were arrested in the forest, where they were indulging in illegal mining. Environmentalists were lamenting the fact that this beautiful biodiversity icon was being decimated every day, under the gaze of everybody, especially the numerous authorities in charge of the protection of the environment, the most well-known among them is the Environmental Protection Agency (EPA), whose offices are numerous across the national territory. EPA is really inefficient, but delving into that will require a full article on its own. Many incoherencies come into play here: the media reports that in 2021, 65 illegal miners or *galamseyers* who claimed to be members of the state security were arrested. These fraudsters had heavy equipment and logistics, and lethal weapons, as I mentioned initially, and most of the time, they were simply "neutralized" by local residents. But the surprising thing is: why was the government or the department directly in charge of the fight against this crime doing nothing? In most cases, people were told that the arrested "national security officers" have been handed over to the police for further investigation, and everything ended there. This is the narration of the pitiful criminal operation of one of such groups: "The suspects invaded the reserve in Akyem-Akateng with a Toyota Land Cruiser under the guise of embarking on an operation to clamp down on *galamseyers* on Tuesday, May 4, 2021. With the help of the community members and forest guards, the tires of the V8 in which the alleged security operatives were driving were deflated. The damaged vehicles included Tundra with registration number NR 9706-20, a Toyota Hilux with registration number GT 9683-14, and a Nissan Patrol GR with registration number GW 1966-12. According to the Asamankese Divisional Police Commander, ACP Kankam Boadu, the suspects were moved to the Eastern Regional Police Command to continue with investigations. Rumor contended that top officials in the government "use", control, support, and protect these National Security officers cum bandits.

The more national security service officers are involved in one way or another in illegal or criminal activities, the more the reputation and efficacy of the law enforcement service itself are undermined. It therefore does not come as a surprise when 2 years after the Atewa Forest scuffle, three young people were arrested for allegedly attacking police officers in the Western Region of the country. The weapons retrieved from the 3 young men were of an astonishing robustness, and it is very difficult to imagine how they could have had such arms if law enforcement or "barons and untouchable tycoons" were not supporting and equipping them. These lines from the Ghanaian media attest the fact that a complicity certainly lies behind the so-called attack: "Public Affairs of the Police said on March 9, 2023, that the Axim Divisional Police Patrol Team reported an attack on the team by a gang that allegedly seized the magazine of a service rifle together with some mobile phones belonging to the police officers... It was said that a pump-action shotgun, two machetes, and eight BB refilled cartridges were retrieved from the suspects' unregistered Honda CV vehicle". Many more items were listed, and as usual, such coverages ended up in a travesty of investigation by the same police. Three reasons could explain this state of affairs: the police are corrupt, utilized by political parties, and ill-trained. It is no secret that all security forces or services in Ghana have been operating for years on a "protocol" recruitment policy, which means that the recruits are simply youngsters who have acquaintances or relatives who are either politically influential or financially well endowed, so in most cases, a certain amount of money is the requirement, the "criterion" for aptitude. This is a sure recipe for the production of an incompetent national security service. The armed forces claimed their innocence and distanced themselves from such illegalities, but that had to be investigated, since many sources contended the opposite of such utterances.

More and more tragedies that expose the jaundiced-faced characteristic of law enforcement in Ghana abound: A suspect apprehended around the period of this scandal allegedly claimed that he is an informant and threatened to reveal key National Security officials who are into illegal mining. This issue was certainly quashed on the spot. All these led a worked up blogger to voice her anger in this language of visual imagery, which summarizes how all the resources of the country are being traded by politicians and their thugs, in search for money to fund their political campaign: "...two of the nation's foreign exchange earners, gold and cocoa are under siege, our forest is under unmitigated depletion, our lands are under attack and our water bodies are in muddied death throes while corruption is at a sure optimum surge in need of radical surgery....the shady conundrum of campaign finance is a real corruption octopus with *galamsey* tentacles and systemic cover-ups". The Aisha Huang syndrome (Aisha Huang was the Chinese galamsey queen of Ghana) was therefore continuing its journey, accumulating more grandeur and doubtlessly compiling the woes of the country.

AFRICANS ARE NOT INSENSITIVE TO THE
TRANSATLANTIC SLAVE TRADE

Chattel slavery is an act and a fact that is visited over and over again. Almost all races have, in one way or another, heard, said and pondered over the Transatlantic slave trade. Those who are directly involved in this discourse are continental Africans and Black diasporans, and that group comprises mainly African Americans and Black Caribbeans. Although impressive scholarly work exists on the realities of chattel slavery, like the various territories that witnessed the capture, sale, revolts, executions, etc., in Africa and the Americas. The dicey idea, opinion and statement in the discussion around the transatlantic slave trade is what emerges when some Black diasporans often contend that the transatlantic slave trade is not much of a concern among continental Africans. In other words, some African Americans and black Caribbean people believe that Africans do not consider slavery as an event that deserves much attention; such persons often take offence at what they find to be the fact that Africans are insensitive to the slave trade. I think that what such black diasporans react to, when they make such comments is the fact that race, racism and its manifestations and consequences are not perceived or handled in the same manner by Africans and Black Diasporans. There is no doubt that these 3 factors are of vital importance to Blacks in the Americas, the Caribbean, Europe and other parts of the world where Black diasporas exist. For instance, African Americans live in the constant fear of the cruel and brutal repression meted out by white America. The mass incarceration of Blacks in the US and on the other side of the Atlantic in general is obvious, and that "black-phobia" culminated in historic injustices and barbaric acts like the murder of so many blacks, to such an extent that many movements were born, in order to lament, immortalize and condemn the act: Black Lives Matter is the most recent of such socio-political movements and the killing of George Floyd in Minneapolis in 2020 is one of the most telling manifestations of that vulnerability of blacks in America. Many more blacks who have committed no crime are killed in the hands of white police officers in the US. Jim Crow and its consequences are still present in education, access to health care, etc. All these contribute to making the slave trade a permanent and indelible horror that the Black diasporans in general live with. As a result, to almost all black diasporans, race, racism, race-based violence, injustice, and many more deadly inequalities are the daily reality of these diasporans. That motivates many of them to embark on projects like returning to their roots, connecting or re-connecting with their "Africanness" through trips to Africa, rebaptizing themselves and taking African names and dropping what slave masters imposed on them. African couture and dressing style, African languages, dances and many factors are therefore patronized or embraced as the key to salvation, the repossession of one's real identity, one's soul by blacks in the diaspora. To crown it all, "pilgrimages" to the slave castles on the West African coast are always done by Black Diasporans. Cape Coast Castle and Elmina Castle in Ghana and the island of Gorée in Senegal are the main ones, known to and visited by those "returnees" who experience high emotions during such trips.

Now it is not accurate to say that continental Africans are insensitive to the slave trade, or that they do not take the transatlantic slave trade with much importance or seriousness. What cannot be denied is that Africa and the Black diaspora have gone through experiences that are different, and as a result, the black race on the continent and outside the continent, especially in the diaspora, have reactions that differ when it comes to issues of race, racism, racial segregation, and the drawbacks of such phenomena. Sadly enough, civil wars, national development, postcolonialism, postcoloniality, and famine are terms and cases that resonate with life in Africa more than the slave trade and its repercussions. That does not mean in any way that slavery and its horrible aftermath are neglected by Africans; it simply means that those difficulties that are part of the daily life of the Black Diasporan are not recurrent in the life of continental Africans. One can even say without any doubt that Africans see the transatlantic slave trade as a preoccupation. Blatant illustrations of that consciousness lie in a close observation of the slave castles on the West African Coast, and what happens inside those castles. While Black Diasporans see in those castles the perfect illustration of the beginning and continuation of their suffering, let us remain mindful of the efforts that Africans put in keeping those slave castles and running them in such a way that the slave trade is permanently engraved in the psyche of the African, the peoples on whose soil those forts are located. The tour guides are very familiar with all the details of chattel slavery, and take Black Diasporans and anybody who desires to know about that page of black History through a thorough journey, lecture, demonstrations, and explanations in the slave forts. "Visitors" are allowed to enter the prison cells, to experience how it feels like to be caged in such 'holes'. Other projects that deserve praise and ovation are the works of the Ghanaian filmmaker Kwaw Ansah, and his Bisa Aberewa Museum in Sekondi

(Western Region, Ghana). This museum was created to be "one of the largest sculptural representations in clay, wood, cement, paintings, and photographs of personalities whose sacrifices have shaped African history, both within the continent and the diaspora". It was officially inaugurated in July 2019 and has about 2,200 artefacts, sculptural pieces, and photographs of heroes of the African struggle and the African American Civil Rights Movement, as well as other Black personalities in the French, Portuguese, and Spanish Caribbean. These scriptural representations capture events within the slave dungeons in Africa, the toils of the Africans on the slave plantations, and highlight the Civil Rights Movement culminating in the election of the first African American as President of the US. This artist attaches inestimable value to the Arts of the Black world. He is interested in anything pan-African; he has been collecting and preserving African art as far as he can remember, as he says and his attachment to African and African American life and values lies in his founding of Pan-African TV in Ghana, which is dedicated to preserving the history of the Black Race, promoting African values and celebrating Pan African heroes. There could not be a more vigorous way of expressing Black life on the African continent.

Another laudable Black life project is the Nkyinkyin Museum of Ada Foah in Ghana. It was built in 2011 by artist Kwame Akoto-Bamfo, as one of the biggest outdoor museums in Ghana and recreates slave trade with an exact and surreal touch: the chained busts and heads of slaves are molded (some with concrete and others with clay) sit on a muddy land, adjacent a water body where other "craftily reconstructed" slaves have started their journey on the sea. It captures the story of the African slave trade and the finished works can be seen at the Nkyinkyim Museum. What reiterates the diasporan dimension of this Ghanaian museum is that some of those sculptures are found at the Legacy Museum, Montgomery, Alabama, USA. The Nkyinkyin symbol means "twisted" and this project aims at capturing the twists and turns in African History. It is important to point out that both the Nkyinkyin and Bisa Aberewa museums are privately funded. They are made and preserved with the money of persons like Kwaw Ansah, Kwame Akoto-Bamfo, and like-minded people. Many other slave forts abound on the coasts of Ghana and more and more slave castles are being discovered and appreciated by Africans and Black Diasporans: while Christianborg Castle in Osu, Accra is well known, Fort Good Hope in Senya, near Accra is being brought to the attention of the international public as well as Fort Amsterdam in Koromantin (Central Region, Ghana) and their function as the most important structures in the transatlantic slave trade is exhibited and coherently linked to the current black consciousness, both in Africa and in the Black Diaspora.

THE CHALLENGE OF THE INTERNATIONAL COURT OF JUSTICE

The International Court of Justice (ICJ) which is also referred to as " the World Court" was established in 1920 and was then "the Permanent Court of International Justice" (PCIJ), a creation of the League of Nations, which itself is the predecessor of the United Nations. In 1945, precisely, the UN Charter renamed the institution the International Court of Justice (ICJ). The body is constituted of 15 judges elected for a 9-year term. Those judges are selected by the UN General Assembly and the Security Council. The Court is the main judicial organ of the UN and its role is twofold: to settle, following international law, legal disputes submitted to it by states and to give advisory opinions on legal questions that are referred to it. The link between the ICJ and the Hague lies in the fact that the various disputes were settled during the late 19th and early 20th century through a medium called "the Hague Conventions," and The Hague in the Netherlands is currently the seat of the court.

The court, therefore, represents a key part of International Law, and records reveal that it has handled 191 cases. Some of the cases are the following: The Corfu Channel Case, filed in 1947 by the United Kingdom, against the People's Republic of Albania, around the issue of state responsibility for damages at sea; the Fisheries Case of 1951 was the culmination of a feud between the UK and Norway, over the exact demarcations of the Norwegian waters and the High Seas for fishing purposes. The Frontier Dispute of 1986 was the dispute between Burkina Faso and the Republic of Mali over a territory between the 2 countries. In 2003, the case dubbed "Oil Platforms" was a contention between the Islamic Republic of Iran and the U.S. because the U.S. Navy allegedly destroyed 3 Iranian oil platforms. More recently, in 2023, in the "Certain Iranian Assets Case", Iran requested the unfreezing and return of 2 billion USD worth of assets that Iran saw to be hers.

The ICJ has a good reputation because of its remarkable and consistent jurisprudence and its independence from political conflicts. That reputation also lies in the fact that it is generally said that since its inception, the court has played a fundamental role in the peaceful resolution and prevention of disputes between states. But between December 2023 and early 2024, the brilliant reputation of the ICJ was in jeopardy; it was about to be changed and for the first time, a case was brought to the court and although no judgment has been passed yet, one of the parties is asking the court to ignore the accusations. These nations are Israel and South Africa. Indeed on October 7, 2023 , the Hamas-led Palestinian militant groups launched an attack against Israeli positions and the casualties were quite sizable:1,139 people, most of whom are Israeli were killed. That started what some media outlets call "the most significant military escalation in the region, since the Yom Kippur War" or the 1973 Arab-Israeli War. Israel's reaction to the attack by Hamas was swift and brutal: the Hamas militants on Israeli land were "cleared", and aerial bombardments and land operations ravaged the lives of Palestinians. International society witnessed one of the cruelest gestures in world history: newborn babies were rescued from hospitals in the Gaza Strip and flown to Egypt where they received treatment, and some were in incubators. Nothing can explain this muscular violence against babies. In December the same year, South

Africa launched a case against Israel, accusing the country of subjecting Palestinians to genocide in its military campaign in Gaza. This does not come as a surprise, when one hears that such a complaint was lodged by South Africa, a country which is very sensitive to violence and discrimination based on race, religion and other "insignificant" features. The violence meted out to the inhabitants of the Gaza Strip reminds many people of the violence that blacks and colored people suffered at the hands of white oppressors, during the Apartheid era in South Africa. Israel's reaction within such a context was following an insensitive and bloodthirsty path, since the country was bent on totally annihilating Hamas regardless of the consequences. So, Israel allegedly responded to those "allegations" with disgust and called the accusations a "blood libel" which should be rejected by the International Court of Justice. The Achilles heel of the ICJ is its inability to enforce judgments and that causes delays in its missions of arbitration. That might explain South Africa's request for a ceasefire, declared by the ICJ in the following few days. The treatment of the Palestinians in the Gaza Strip is equated to genocide by several analysts who buttress their judgment or opinion with the following derogatory comments made by high Israeli military officials: the defense minister Yoav Gallant referred to Palestinians as "human animals". One general of the Israeli army is known to have made a comment that is in line with that of the minister and sticks to the animalization of Palestinians. The army general states that "human animals must be treated as such. There will be no electricity, and no water in Gaza. There will only be destruction. You wanted hell, you will get hell."

Africa's involvement in this conflict also transpired in the acceptance of an African country to take in Palestinians, away from the war zone and the Democratic Republic of Congo (DRC) is that country. Israel was said to have held secret talks with the authorities of the DRC to accommodate Palestinians since literally no land will be left for them [Palestinians] to farm and build houses on. On the other hand, Rwanda was refuting information that states that the country is in favor of taking in Palestinians. Rwanda called that a "disinformation" emanating from Israeli media. No country remains indifferent to the carnage against Palestinians in the Gaza Strip. While some nations contend that Israel was carrying out a crime similar to anti-semitism in many ways, others certainly were in support of the Israeli camp. It is obvious that the US is one of the biggest players in this tragic "game". In their direct interactions with Israel, the US offer a vast array of sophisticated weapons. At the diplomatic level, the US make it impossible to take any measure or decision that goes against the interests of their ally, Israel.

NEW LANGUAGE AND IDENTITY IN KUMASI (GHANA)

Language is a key component of Identity. The language of a people or a society says who they are, what their practices and belief systems among others revolve around. Language varies based on the changes that society undergoes. It would not be too far-fetched to say that language is a mirror of society. One phenomenon emerged in Ghana, precisely in Kumasi, the commercial hub of the country in the early 2000s and was popularized in 2020. The youth speak a new language called 'SAKA" and a category of young people also claim to be living in 'KUMERICA' (America in Kumasi), a kind of society which has its own codes. The 'Kumaricans' sing in a language called 'Asakaa' a derivative of Saka, the swapped form of 'kasa' which is the word for "to speak" in Twi, one of the main languages in Ghana; Twi is the language of the Ashanti, the majority of the residents in Kumasi.

Ingenious Linguistic Construction and Impressive Hybrid Music

The Ghanaian youth amazes many with their creativity and ingenuity. In Kumasi, they craftily manipulate languages and music genres through borrowing(s) and combinations in order to create their own language and music.

Saka or Keshey

Saka is a slang which epitomizes youngsters' desire for a new linguistic/ language identity. The name comes from the Twi word Kasa, which means "to speak." So, this code name 'Saka' is now a slang which is quickly becoming an alternative to the pidgin language. Saka is called Keshey in the High School milieu and this slang mixes sounds from Twi (mainly) and English also into unique words. This new language which is the pride of the Kumasi boys has no exclusive alphabet and no definitive sounds. The main rule or secret is for the speaker to be smart enough to interchange sounds and articulate swiftly. A student put it in these terms: 'It's like when you have a word, you just take the first pronunciation [sound], take the back one and bring it forward. So you just change it and you have to speak it fast and when you are saying it, you have to change it in your mind fast'. The reason behind the coinage of Saka is that in Ghana in general, and in Accra in particular, almost everybody speaks pidgin, and the Kumasi youth want to distinguish themselves through their own language, Saka or Keshey. What started as a mere street code is now a symbol of pride that many people in Kumasi yearn to be associated with, especially high school students. The prestige of the street code turned language is reflected in the admiration and desire that this Kumasi gentleman expresses: 'I feel attracted to the Keshey, I have the passion to learn but it feels difficult to learn it. Sometimes, when I see my friends speaking that particular language, I feel left out. If I see someone speaking it, it's nice and the way they speak it is very good.' The 'value' of Keshey increased during the 2021 National Science and Math Quiz, when the supporters of the team from Kumasi were speaking; that earned those speakers a great deal of admiration. It is almost unimaginable what a special place this language occupies in people's hearts. They pray that it flourishes and spreads in the 2 big cities of Ghana, starting from its source, Kumasi, as this statement shows: 'Our prayer is that God will help us to give the children and the elderly people the knowledge to speak the language because it is now becoming the whole thing in Kumasi; some of the Accra people also speak the language.'

Kumerica Subculture

In the year 2020, a group of young men from Kumasi went viral for their aggressive and hard-hitting music as well as their accompanying videos, which bore a striking resemblance to the rap videos coming out of America some 10 years earlier. Rap music is nothing new to Ghana, which has seen the rise of many local stars in the last couple of years, but there is something different about the latest movement from Kumasi that has brought international recognition to the 'Kumerica' subculture. Whilst the songs are partly spoken in English, they also feature both Twi, which can easily be understood in Ghana, as a dialect of Akan, and new Kumerican slang, which is effectively a form of Twi code that sees the first and last parts of words swapped, or Saka.

Kumerican artists add an 'A' on both sides of the word, and get the name of the new rap subgenre they created, which is 'Asakaa'. The word Kumerica itself is a 'mash-up' of Kumasi, the city these young rappers hail from, and America, the country that has inspired much of the new culture. It has primarily influenced the fashion and sound of youth in the Ashanti region of Ghana, but through its regular presence in the region's music, the circulation of the term finally became much more prevalent across Ghana and the world. Stars of Asakaa confirm that the uniqueness of their music lies in their use of local language and their unique street terms, something that is pretty much the norm with new rap music. Another striking feature of Asakaa is that this music is a harmonious blend of Kumasi realities and the American influences embraced by the artists who are honest enough to say that their sounds are not uniquely theirs. This new music carries a very distinctive American influence that is noticeable from the common "Woo's" and growling adlibs that featured heavily in the recent Brooklyn-based drill movement, but Asaaka mixes that with a local sound and style to create an experience that stands out against their international competition. One of the most popular songs, which seemed to have made Kumerica's presence known, was the posse cut "Sore," which is Twi for "wake up." It sees 19-year-old Yaw Tog alongside other Ghanaian talented artists like O'Kenneth, Reggie, City Boy, and Jay Bahd, rap about their experiences on the streets of Kumasi.

Whilst Asakaa and Kumasi's most popular rappers are a big part of what Kumerica has become known for, the concept of Kumerica is much greater and covers more than music. Numerous suburbs in Kumasi are now increasingly referred to as different locations in the US, and every important area in Kumasi is given the name of a state or a big city in the US. For example, Manhyia (the royal palace in Kumasi) is commonly referred to as Washington, D.C., Abrepo is Georgia, Abuakwa is Chicago, etc. Furthermore, Kumerica has its own flag, with the following colors: yellow (Kumasi is the reservoir of mineral resources), green (the city is referred to as the Garden City in Ghana), and black (Black pride, the hope of the motherland). The designer chooses the pattern of the colors.

Kumerica residents stress that Kumerica, Asakaa, Saka, and Keshey do not have any tribal, separatist, or political intention. They emphasize its contribution to Ghanaian culture and ask that the language Saka or Asaaka be added to the list of national languages studied in Ghanaian schools.

INEXPLICABLE EPISODE IN BURKINA FASO INSECURITY

The Al-Qaeda backed attacks against civilians in Burkina Faso started in 2015 and revolved like graphs, with ups and downs. This mysterious conflict whose origin no one can pinpoint seemed to have come to stay. This tragic development is really macabre and damaging since Burkina was one of the most peaceful and stable countries in West Africa. The UNHCR would send refugees there for their safety, and international summits would be hosted in Ouagadougou, the capital city. That persisted for decades, to such an extent that both national and international opinion were accusing the then President, Blaise Compaoré of pretension, as someone who is interested in the image of his country in the eyes of international observers, rather than engaging the problems in the country. He certainly was a stooge of France, but violence was not known in Burkina, and no one could predict the current descent into hell that has gotten hold of the country of the incorruptible Man.

When the terrorist attacks burgeoned in 2015, many thought that it would be a brief period of instability, but unfortunately, events took a completely different turn. The tragedy kept augmenting in magnitude; more than half of the national territory was no longer controlled by the national authorities, several thousands of people were killed and an equally colossal number were internally displaced and became familiar with the panoply of discomfort that ensues this type of insecurity. Two (2) coups d'état were caused by the insecurity since the army found the civilian regime of former President Roch Kaboré to be either incapable of defeating the terrorists or indifferent to the woes of the populations. The second pronunciamento, that of September 2022 brought to power a young army officer who initiated a heated battle against that violent canker and for some time, the terrorists were being defeated. They were killed in large numbers by both regular soldiers and civilian volunteers, with sophisticated weapons purchased from Russia. All in all, the arrival of Captain Ibrahim Traoré on the political scene gave hope to the Burkinabè and all those who are concerned about the security situation in the country. All niches and caches of pro-jihadist combatants and their logistics were severely destroyed. France and the UN experienced a sudden shake-up in their relations with Burkina, since many paths of terrorist activities were traced to France and the UN.

What happened on April 20, 2023 took almost all by surprise: the media reports that 147 persons were rounded up and executed by the Burkinabè army. That did set minds racing, wildly: is the Burkinabè army now killing those whom their duty is to protect? Others were wondering if a pro-terrorist faction had emerged within the Burkinabè army, and many more speculations were made. The unforeseen carnage is one of those cruel brutalities that are classified in general as 'indescribable crimes', due to its gory, traumatic and inhumane features. This is a summary of the events of that early morning in Karma, a village in the north of the country: "On 20 April, in Karma, a village 15 km from Ouahigouya in the north of the country, elements of the Burkinabè army entered the village at 7.30 in the morning, in what villagers believed to be a routine patrol.

The soldiers rounded the inhabitants up, collected their identity documents, and then shot the villagers at point-blank range, killing at least 147 people. The attack lasted from 7.30 in the morning until 2 in the afternoon." It was a real 'stab in the back' because the national army had gradually succeeded in gaining the trust and support of the civilians. So, seeing national troops in the vicinity rather made the civilians think that their most reliable allies and protectors were around.

The implication of the national army in this massacre is almost obvious, because everything about these perpetrators led the populations to believe that they were troops of a special and well-known unit of the army, the 3rd Battalion of the Rapid Intervention Brigade (BIR). Sadly enough, 45 children were among the casualties, and the victims hailed from several neighborhoods, certainly because of the usual friendly and trustworthy rapport between the people and the troops. Unfortunately, the April 20 encounter was one of betrayal.

Amnesty International tried to make sense of this deadly fracas, and exchanges with survivors revealed that the soldiers executed the civilians because to them, these civilians facilitated, some days before, the movement of jihadist groups that attacked the army and Volunteers for the Defense of the Homeland (VDP). The fact that the perpetrators insisted on checking the ID of the civilians before shooting them certainly means a lot: did they want to make sure they were face-to-face with Burkinabè civilians and not Al-Qaeda terrorists? Were these elements of the 3rd BIR some sympathizers of the jihadists, on an execution operation against Burkinabè civilians who rather needed help? Had this unit of the Burkinabè national army turned against their civilian compatriots? Or were the soldiers retaliating against civilian populations whom they thought had facilitated the passage of jihadist terrorists at some point and as such they were to pay for that act? The following lines seem to buttress that last hypothesis: "When they [the military] arrived, they asked to check our IDs. Then they told us to bring out the women and children so that they could check theirs too. They gathered us together to speak to us. They asked us why we were still in the village, when the surrounding villages were deserted. We said that it was the terrorists who had ordered the inhabitants of those villages to leave. They hadn't given us any such ultimatum, and we didn't want to leave our land. And they [the military] said, 'Since you fear the terrorists more than us, we're going to treat you like the terrorists do.' (…) They told the men to remove everything they had on them (mobiles, IDs, and money), and then they surrounded us and indicated to certain people that they should go to a given place". The civilians were certainly all shot at the indicated spot. Was the carnage of Karma then a barbaric blind and illegal act of military vengeance?

The scars are deep and indelible and the trauma doubtlessly left innocent people incapacitated (to some extent) for life as one of the few survivors' states: "I managed to survive by covering myself with the blood of the bodies that were right next to me. It was the Burkina Faso military that committed this massacre. A man who saw his 72-year-old brother and many other victims being shot says he finds it difficult to eat. He is shocked, traumatized and cannot come to terms with the pain. He adds that seeing the bullet-ridden bodies of women and children, made him cry and vomit".

Serious investigations must be conducted since this sudden brutal and ambiguous twist might be hiding other dangerous intentions.

TRIBULATIONS OF THE AFRICAN YOUTH: KÉMI SÉMA, THE HOPE IN THE TUMULT

Not much needs to be said, to express the state in which the African youth find themselves , especially in this era, the 2020 onwards: while some refer to them as a generation of martyrs, others see them as a sacrificed, lost or mortgaged generation, all this because of the multifaceted nature of the woes this group of young people face. They are often blamed for being non-patriotic because their dearest wish is to leave the shores of Africa, in perilous condition, in an attempt to join Europe and sometimes, cross over to America. Unemployment on the continent is the most poisonous obstacle the African youth faces. That big monster has a cohort of malaise like the high cost of living, unjust treatment since they see a few openly ingurgitating the wealth of the nation, a heart-wrenching phenomenon that former Burkinabè President decries in these terms: " for so long, the grain of the poor has fattened the cow of the rich". This cul-de-sac seems to offer no chance of reversing or a U-turn and pushes some students to drop out of college, since there is no job after all. That defeatist attitude is over erased when lecturers counsel such students and show them what looks like the most reasonable option. To stay in school, get a degree (s), and then look for a job. Of course not all of them are successfully convinced by such words. In French speaking Africa where private enterprise is less developed than it is among Anglophones, the best brains of most societies resigned themselves to the jobs that the IMF and its suicidal SAPs imposed: from the High School graduates to the Master degree holders, the salvation resided in competing for jobs like teachers, nurses and few other categories of clerks. Some youngsters caught up is another category in this rat race. Those who held no degree that could fetch them any of the very few jobs or posts pre-destined to the children of a few rich of manipulated politicians who sold their conscience to a certain couplet dubbed France-Afrique or African Democracy. Those who had nothing to lose and would often embark on the most dangerous of adventures. Dambisa Moyo's *Dead Aid* opens with the voice of two boys from that class. The extremely pitiful tragedy is posed this way in words very difficult to peruse: "To the Excellencies and officials of Europe: We suffer enormously in Africa. Help us. We have problems in Africa. We lack rights as children. We have war and illness, we lack food…We want to study, and we ask you to help us study so we can be like you, in Africa." Message found on the bodies of Guinean teenagers Yaguiné Koita and Fodé Tounkara, stowaways who died attempting to reach Europe in the landing gear of an airliner. The date was August 2, 1999, and the boys aged 14 and 15 had died of cold and lack of oxygen and were trying to escape poverty by relocating to Europe. At an altitude of 10,000 Km, they had no chance to survive, although they had wrapped themselves up in layers of heavy clothing, clinging onto the landing gear of the Belgian Sabena aircraft. Their choice might have been motivated by a previous similar attempt carried out by a young Senegalese who survived the perilous journey and reached Lyon in France. Although I do not subscribe to the belief of the Euro-American Eldorado, I perfectly understand the choice of these very young boys. The most complex dreams that cross the mind of someone their age is doing what they did. The most painful aspect in this equation is the fact that two decades after that "atrocious event" as the Western media called it, conditions in Africa have obviously worsened. The daily occurrence in the overage West African country today is one or several of the following: vertiginous inflation, massive unemployment, naked pitiful or gluttonous corruption, famine, diseases, constant insecurity, civil wars, jihadist attacks, and much more. Everyone has certainly wondered many times, when the cycle will break.

The voice that gives hope to the youth and every politico-social mind in Africa and beyond is Kémi SÉBA, the 31-year-old French young man born to immigrants from Benin. Born Stellio Gilles R. C. Chichi, his name Kémi SÉBA is the Egyptian for Black Star. While he was simply referred to as a "French Beninese" some years ago, he is a force to reckon with today, and is known as a pan-Africanist political leader and geopolitical journalist, and one would not be wrong to refer to him as one of the most prominent (civilian) figures of anti-colonialist resistance in Francophone Africa. His curiosity and rejection of passive conformism is noticed when at age 18,when he joins the US based- Nation of Islam (NOI); in his 20s, he pursues his quest and formulates his own ideology" during a visit to Egypt, where he takes the nom de guerre Kémi Séba and became the spokesperson of the Kemite Party, founded in 2002 by Khalid Muhamad, a prominent African American Muslim Minister and activist, and former leading member of the Nation of Islam (who later joined the New Black Panther Party). Kemi Seba gives hope to the African youth today, and his gestures are so grand, brave, selfless, and well-calculated. He promotes Black Identity, on the continent and in the diaspora, bridges the gap of language barriers, and confronts racism, intimidation, and subjugation in any form and anywhere. The Pan-African dimension of his gesture led him to pose unforgettable initiatives in almost all corners of Africa and his main concern is a better present and future for Africa especially the African youth. A self-described "militant defender of the dignity of the Black people", he was imprisoned a couple of times, especially in France, where he trampled over several conservative rules and regulations. That rather reinvigorate is tenacity and encouraged him to move to Senegal, where he continued his political activism and became a lecturer in African universities and, from 2013, a political columnist in various African television channels. That earned him a certain popularity among the French-speaking African youth, who could then clearly see him as someone committed to the defense of African sovereignty. In 2008 he was a key member of the Movement of the "Wretched" of Imperialism (*Mouvement des Damnés de l'Impérialisme*) and his most meritorious action so far is his rejection of the CFA franc and the attempt to replace it with the Eco that would be the currency of ECOWAS. He showed that anti-imperialist position by burning in public in Senegal CFA franc banknotes and that was a slap in the face of all pro-France governments and people. He was jailed for that but continued his crusade once released from jail. In 2019 he accused France of being partly responsible for terrorism in the Sahel and proposed the involvement of the "Pan-African Civilian Volunteers" in the anti-jihadist fight, and placed himself at the service of the regionalist armies in the anti-jihadist struggle. He cautions leaders against fraudulent elections and meets (despite the resistance of conservatives) with some of the young military rulers that are currently emerging in West Africa. He has devoted members and partisans all across Africa, is deeply involved in Civil Society movements and keeps writing and speaking, awakening, fortifying and galvanizing the African and Black youth in general. Some of his most influential publications are the following: Supra-négritude (2013), Black Nihilism (2014) and Obscure Époque (2016). Kémi Séba is the voice that the African youth has to listen to, now. His language is accessible to all walks of life; everybody's woes find their place in his words and primary concerns. Kémi Séba belongs to the crop of activists that Yaguiné Koita and Fodé Tounkara, the deceased Guinean boys were calling for.

CASH CROPS HAMPER LIVELIHOODS IN AFRICA: COTTON IN BURKINA FASO AND HEVEA IN GHANA

The major alternatives that agriculture faces in almost all African countries revolve around two key points: cash crops and food crops. In certain countries like Burkina Faso in West Africa, that tendency started in the 1990s, when planting cotton for exportation to France to manufacture fibers and other products was encouraged over the cultivation of food crops like maize, millet, rice, and many others. Farmers later realized the disaster in such a shift of focus because the practice was simply leading them into indebtedness, and their families and the entire population were experiencing frequent hunger, an enemy that had been almost eradicated by the self-sufficiency agrarian reforms and agricultural policies of Thomas Sankara and the 1983 to 1987 revolution.

When the revolution was truncated in October 1987, the manipulations of France and the impositions of suffocating diktats regained ground, and cotton, the main cash crop of Burkina, which benefited France, was given preference. A little history of that crop takes us back to 1924, when the French colonizers forced Burkinabè (then Voltaïque) farmers into growing cotton. Then in 1949, the French Company for the Production of Fibers and Textile (CFDT) was founded and made to flourish in Burkina because of the Sahelian climate that was conducive for such an activity. Cotton was then produced and conveyed to the harbor of Côte d'Ivoire, where it was shipped to France. The produce was conveyed from one French colony to another, and no hurdle stood in the way. All the benefits went to France, and the populations of the then Upper Volta were left with just a few clerical and mechanical jobs, and also seasonal employment for poor youth. Some years down the line, a semblance of nationalism and "Africanization" was imposed on the cotton economy, and the name of the company was changed to Society for the Production of Fibers and Textiles (SOFITEX), a name and acronym that dropped the word "France" and no substantial transformation was carried out. The goal of the company was still the same: to ensure the supply of cotton and textiles to France. The period of subtle and dangerous exploitation in the cotton industry coincided with 1990s (at the peak of the World Bank's Structural Adjustment   Programs, SAPs) and was marked by more aggressiveness in the cotton production: money was lent to farmers and they were encouraged to grow more cotton, pesticides and other agricultural chemicals were loaned to them with ease, to such an extent that the majority of farmers turned away from growing food crops and bought into the main cash crop, which is cotton. It might help to mention that the main exports of Burkina were then cotton and meat. Harvest time was a moment of rude awakening when the same farmers were made to sell their produce to the CFDT to refund the debts. All the money obtained from the sale of the cotton was given back to the company in that reimbursement process. That vicious cycle went on unabated for years, and it is still going on.

Currently, European, North American, and Australian industrial mining companies are embarking on a similar or more brutal practice, which encourages farmers and land owners to sell their land. The production of food crops reduces and the race for money from gold (and the gold mining companies) is the luxurious and coveted activity; a kind of "gold rush" settled in, with all its inconvenience (drug use, violence, diseases, crimes, etc.) but the overage Burkinabè citizen believes that the mining companies brought more salvation and benefit than harm.

In neighboring Ghana, a similar situation is occurring, although with differences due to the climate and natural resources in Ghana: the forest, mineral resources, the sea, and the cash crop, which the country is known for, cocoa, all play a game similar to the one prevailing in the less naturally endowed neighbor, Burkina Faso. Not much was heard about cash crops or gold mining companies threatening food production agriculture, until recently, when small-scale gold mining, industrial Western companies exploiting gold, and the Chinese involvement in that sector were discussed. This is really what is becoming the nightmare of the conscientious Ghanaian. The debauchery that comes with gold mining in Burkina is the same in Ghana. But now, the situation in Ghana is morphing into a more complicated one that could have more drastic and negative impacts: cocoa production is now being threatened by rubber production, a phenomenon that is not so much noticed, although communities complain once in a while. Growing Hevea Brasiliensis leads to rubber production, and that chain of agro-industrial activity is controlled by Western companies, which, like all societies of that sort, operate on a straight capitalistic principle: profit and profit alone, no matter what the nefarious repercussions are. In the area that is called the Western Region of Ghana, precisely near the city of Takoradi a solidly implanted rubber producing company called Ghana Rubber Estates Limited (GREL) a company in which the government of Ghana currently holds 25% of the shares, has been operating since 1957 (approximately) grows Hevea and turns the produce into rubber which is sold in many parts of the world. Michelin, the French giant tyre manufacturing company, has close links with GREL.

Documents that exhibit results of studies conducted by the Environmental Protection Agency (EPA) of Ghana tell citizens that no negative impact of the agro-industrial business falls on the populations. The study rather shows that mitigating measures have been put in place to control and counter, neutralize all those disadvantages. People are told that benefits like employment, health care facilities, schools, etc., are what the neighboring communities get from the operation of the company. But in another part of the country, the Eastern Region, precisely Asikasu, a small farming community of about 10,000 people, the same Hevea cultivation and rubber production is a serious source of worry to residents: 4,900 acres (2,000 hectares) of farms have been "destroyed" to make way for rubber plantations. Cocoa was grown on half of that land, and plantain, coconut, orange, maize, and other crops on the land were also destroyed," as farmers put it. There are other stories of such destruction to make way for rubber plantations in other parts of the same region (around the Upper West Akyem, Suhum, and Ayensua North Districts in the Eastern Region). The rubber-producing company contends that those thousands of hectares of land, some of which included cocoa farms, were acquired from the paramount chief in the affected areas and claim that the farmers were compensated, a statement that the farmers refute. Other farmers have this to say: "In 1995, GREL came to tell us that the government of Ghana asked them to bring us rubber trees. They said that one acre of rubber was more profitable than 10 acres of cocoa. They told us that everyone needs to grow rubber trees to wipe out poverty. So, they made us cut down our cocoa, coconut, cassava, and oranges".

The result is total disenchantment for these Ghanaian farmers, like the Burkinabè cotton producer, to some extent: The financial benefit of cocoa production is no more there, poverty settles in, environmental drawbacks like the unbearable odor of rubber plantation make life difficult for populations, and to crown it all, the soil is negatively affected. Research shows that the soil on which Hevea was grown is permanently reduced to non-cultivable land because all its nutrients are sucked up. The same company, GREL, owns the rubber production both in the Eastern and the Western regions of Ghana. It is incongruous to see the ineffectiveness of their activity in the Eastern Region of the country, when only good things are cited about their activities in the Western Region.

The disturbing fact here is that a very precious and income-generating cash crop, which is almost synonymous with the name and pride of Ghana, is being neglected by agents or institutions that are backed up by the state in most cases. A country that achieved its Millennium Development Goal by reducing hunger prevalence from 40.5 % of the population in 1993 to less than 5% in 2013 is now crawling back into the same pit.

BILL GATES AND AFRICA'S GROWING POPULATION

Africa's population represents a genuine threat to many and for several reasons. The West dreads the power that the exponential growth of Africa's population is. Statistics pose that 40% of Africans were below 15 years in 2023. This is a contrast with the white population of Europe and the US that has been experiencing a thinning growth rate for decades. Cultural preferences are some of the reasons behind this dichotomy between the African scene and that of the West. While it is generally believed that in Africa, one's children are one's social security (unlike the West), developed nations treasure the comfort, privacy and pleasure that come with a childless couple. A statement trending on social media about 2 years ago attributes the following view to former US President, Donald Trump, after his "shit hole" scandalous comparison: "Africans are good at only one thing which is marrying several spouses and giving birth to many children". This view might not be that of the average Westerner but it is obvious that the demographic explosion on the African continent sends chills down the spine of the West, for several reasons.

The current opinion, behavior, belief and action of African societies is a result of the change that occurred on the continent. The majority of the population is the youth who are attached to social media, can verify the authenticity of information, a generation that rebels against the subjugation that their parents and grandparents went through in the hands of Westerners. That causes drastic and bitter changes in European societies whose profits, superiority myth and disguised parasite-like relation with Africa are revealed in broad daylight.

Europeans are now wondering how their existence will be possible without the oil, gas, uranium and many mineral resources that were pillaged from Africa. The rejection of European domination by African countries is a 360-degree movement that can be explained by one factor only: an increasing African population that will experience a real "explosive" augmentation in the next 10 to 20 years. That means unimaginable misery of diverse types for Europe and the US.

The digital affinity that pervades every corner of the world makes it easy for conscientious commentators and analysts to air their views and one of those who have taken upon themselves to ponder over the situation in Africa is the Cameroonian Nathalie Yamb who tirelessly dissects daily occurrences on the continent, traces the roots of important phenomena and lays bare the possible repercussions. One topic that she spent much time and energy discussing and educating on is the growth of the African population and the actions of some people who pose as philanthropists while their real goal is to annihilate that growth. According the Ms. Yamb, in a reflection she posted on June 24th this year, the US billionaire Bill Gates is in that circle that works to reverse the increasing dynamics of the African population. To the political analyst, the American billionaire uses stratagems like medical assistance mainly in the form of vaccines. She adds that India is also a victim of this well-planned annihilation project, since the population of that country is already gargantuan and keeps increasing by leaps and bounds. The core of this piece is the case of Africa.

Nathalie Yamb whose posts and arguments are accessible to anyone who cares to read them, and her meticulously researched progressist and Pan-Africanist "lectures" and those of chroniclers, researchers and activists like Alain Foka, Kemi Seba and many others are legion. The lady does not mince words and clearly refers to Bill Gates as a silent indefatigable militant of the depopulation mission of Africa. She discloses that the billionaire is the main financier of the Global Alliance for Vaccines and Immunization (GAVI), a body that is commonly labeled as a "public-private global health partnership with the goal of increasing access to immunization in poor countries". This "corporation" is credited with the immunization of almost half of the world's children, a gesture that prevents more than 13 million deaths world-wide. It is further praised as a business-oriented and technology-focused entity, ranked well-above the World Health Organization (WHO). So, the mission that GAVI assigns to itself is to provide vaccine to "beggar countries" for the immunization of their populations.

The DPT or DTP vaccine is another useful element in the illustration of Bill Gates's hidden agenda, according to Yamb. This one is a combination vaccine against three infectious diseases in humans: Diphtheria, Pertussis (whooping cough), and Tetanus (lockjaw). This vaccine has been banned in the USA and Europe since the 1980s, due to its severe side-effects. According to the analyst, since that period (the 1980s), Bill Gates financed the immunization of 161 million African children with DPT. The same source points out that the US billionaire solicited the assistance of the Danish government in this philanthropic immunization mission. The Danish requested a scientific proof of the efficiency of the vaccine and since Bill Gates could not provide it, the Danish conducted their own investigations and unearthed the following diabolic facts: the death rate of African girls vaccinated with the anti-DTP product was 10 times higher than that of their counterparts who were not administered the vaccine. Although the vaccinated ones were protected against Diphtheria and Tetanus, they usually succumbed more often from ailments like anemia, malaria, pneumonia and other respiratory diseases.

A more recent plan of the duo Gates/GAVI is the COVAX initiative, which our analyst calls "criminal". The initiative aimed at distributing millions of AstraZeneka Covishield doses, made for the "immunization" of Africans. In this case, the type destined for blacks was never authorized in Europe and the one allegedly made for whites was removed from the pharmacy shelves due to its side effects. Africans refused the vaccine and while Gates was expecting the death of millions of Africans, Africa emerged as the least affected continent by the pandemic. The same source adds that such examples are uncountable on the billionaire's path. In Nigeria, Cameroon, almost everywhere in Africa and India, vaccines supposedly manufactured against polio, HIV/AIDS, uterine cancer and malaria rather aim to kill populations that represent a threat in the eyes of the West. Ms. Yamb does not hide her disappointment in the billionaire whom she calls "a psychopath disguised as a philanthropist working to reduce the population of the third world". In all this, the solace comes from the negligence that African countries exhibited towards a trio that Nathalie Yamb finds to be a nuisance: GAVI / Bill Gates, France and the E U. Only President Paul Kagame of Rwanda and three other leaders attended the forum they organized. Countries that collaborate with the Bill Gates Foundation, GAVI and others, and accept vaccines coming as aid from the West are simply endangering the health of their populations. The dearest wish of Westerners is an "African continent without Africans" and here is the proof according to Ms.

Yamb: in the US and Europe, children are immunized with DTPa, a variant of DTP with less side effects while DTP, conversely, is still being shipped to Africa. Her last piece of advice to Africans is to avoid Mosquirix, which is said to be a vaccine against malaria, donated to Africa by "kind-hearted" Western pharmaceutical laboratories. I still wonder why Bill Gates indulges in such a horrible project which is the anti-thesis of what his foundation is known for, world-wide. Of course he lives in the West, precisely at the heart of mercantilism and merciless profit-making ventures but wealth could be amassed without a homicide-driven agenda.

RELATIONS BETWEEN FRANCE AND AFRICA: URGENT NEED FOR PARADIGM CHANGE

A discussion that brought together two French analysts posed the very urgent need to recalibrate the current tumultuous rapport between Africa and France. The key points of that debate deserve more reflection and praxis. One needs to ponder once again which new path has the potential to lead to those novel dynamics in the relations between Africa and France.

One thing that cannot be underrated is that Africa, especially French-speaking Africa, is going through a new "decolonization", one that comes after that of the 1960s. France is not wanted in her former colonies; they cry for a rupture in the relations between them and France, and that new decolonization is a systemic fracture. It germinated, matured, and expressed itself rationally and scientifically; no miracle is behind it, and one could see it coming. Certain elements paved the way for that new decolonization, which in itself calls for a revision or re-evaluation of relations between Africa and France. The demographic architecture of Africa is the opposite of that of France. While more youthful exuberance is the main trait of the African population, which is less than 35 years old in its vast majority, the demographic composition of France is the reverse. Citizens beyond 35 years old represent the vast majority. That age bracket is synonymous with more careful moves, a fear of certain things like risk-taking actions or movements, and a generation that is more "conservative" and less open to change. That difference in the demographic patterns informs the buoyant changes coming from Africa today, changes that call for a new France-Africa rapport. Social media added to that wind of new dynamics, and Francophone Africa's call for a change could not be muffled: it was loud, emanating from the hearts of concerned citizens, and the call knew what it was aspiring for. One new factor in today's Africa is that no source is the sole owner of the metanarrative. The youth can verify every utterance and major judgment made or passed by every Western or Western-related source and form their own opinion on what is happening in the world. So, new voices and aspirations are coming from Africa, and for a long time, France did not seem to consider that, hence her utter surprise at the form that Africa-France relations have morphed into.

These new connotations in the discourse, as it is understood and evaluated by Africans today, lead us to a situation where the "emotional" occupies a primordial role. Words, sentiments, and statements made by the French political elite are carefully dissected by the Africans, who, due to their action-oriented posture, do not hesitate to embark upon radical and historic actions and revolutionary movements. That explains the coups and the new diplomatic alliances that followed them. Each rhetoric has the potential to unleash a gigantic corollary. Nothing is taken at face value as it used to be. That era of the "emotive or emotional", which is justified, to me, is the outcome of actions, decisions, and policies that have built up over decades. What the African older generations put up with cannot be accepted by the children and grandchildren of that previous generation.

When one looks at some of the decisions that the Elysée has taken at certain moments, many see that the attitude of France was synonymous with a basic mistake, which could have devastating consequences. A case in point is the 400 Niger youngsters who applied for visas to study in France. The moment was the climax of the fracas between Niamey and Paris. These youngsters were apparently afraid of the prevailing situation in Niger and they could be, according to many analysts those who would be instrumental in the near future in negotiating and constructing the relations between their country and France, after their studies in France. By refusing to grant them visas, France therefore missed a great opportunity. Still on the migration, immigration and visa case, a crucial change occurred in France, under the presidency of Nicholas Sarkozy. Before he was elected president, decisions on entry visas into France were handled by the French Ministry of Foreign Affairs. In other words, allowing people of other nationalities into France was considered a decision that impacts the image of France in the eyes of the world. Under Sarkozy's presidency, these measures became the preoccupation of the French Ministry of the Interior. That could mean that France is less open to the movement of people in general between France and the outside world. Those who became victims of that measure were mainly citizens of the Maghreb and sub-Saharan Francophone Africa. That decision snowballed into a decimation of the cooperation between France and Africa. That close scrutiny of the entry into France added to the bad reputation of France in terms of freedom of the movement of people and her anti-racism stand.

According to one of the panelists during the debate I mentioned above, the world is in a context where building relationships between geographical areas is key. Unfortunately, France did a faux pas at that level, too. From 1990 to date, the number of French cooperation workers in Africa has declined by 15%. Of course, much was said about the "unhealthy" or secretive spying function of French cooperation in Africa, but certain good sides could be seen in it, and that closeness with Africa led to socially oriented outcomes that contribute to a bond between France and Africa. Many French cooperation workers and many African students in France founded families, bi-racial couples, and had children who were French-African. That dynamic drastically dropped off late, and ironically, France does not draw any benefit from it. The contrast between France and the USA is more striking at this level: The US seems to know how to use her African diaspora to their advantage. An example is the role played by the US ambassador to Burkina Faso in 2014, when Blaise Compaoré was chased out of power. Ambassador Tulinabo Salama Mushingi is an American of Congolese descent, and many good things are said about his mission in Burkina: some isolated incidents that could have turned into diplomatic incidents were well handled, and troubles were then neutralized. Another feather in the ambassador's cap is how bloodshed was avoided in the rejection of Blaise Compaoré. The US ambassador is said to have played an important role in that historic political occurrence in Burkina. That was a Congolese African, as I said earlier.

Another error that France made was to confuse hegemony and universalism. Their position as former colonizer or hegemonic power turned at some point into a heavy upper hand. Imposition and intimidation were at the core of the rapport between France and Africa, and the African populations today are calling for a fair partnership, an erasure of double standards in issues like human rights and others. China, Saudi Arabia, and other countries should not be exonerated when the juntas in West Africa are constantly "demonized" as violators of human rights.

These are some of the errors that France committed, and she is now paying the price. The survival and prosperity of France are closely linked to her relationship with Africa. One could even say that access to Africa's resources is a sine qua non for France's survival. Political analysts Laurent Bigot and Alain Juillet sum the situation up in the following words: France must re-evaluate or revise her political "software", the core of the machinery regulating her foreign policy, especially her dealings with Africa.

AMBASSADOR ARIKANA: THE MOUTHPIECE OF AFRICA AND THE BLACK DIASPORA IN THE 21ST CENTURY

H.E. Ambassador Dr. Arikana Chihombori-Quao, a physician by profession, has been fighting a ferocious war against the main hurdles that Africa and the Black Diaspora have been facing for almost a century. This medical doctor and activist, native of Zimbabwe, when talking about her career as a great diplomat, states that this journey started as a "game", or a period of attempt that she thought would prove futile: she has worked as a medical doctor all her life, is a female, and is not a diplomat. The proposal to accept the post of African Union (AU) ambassador to the USA was made to her by a friend and colleague, and she thought that she was not cut out for such a position and believed that a semester of work would prove that she must return to her cherished career as a family doctor. Destiny had a different choice for Dr Arikana. She will ultimately find herself performing the job as an excellent ambassador, driven by passion, who marvelously performs beyond the requirements of her job.

One of the first international involvements of Dr Arikana is a medical Pan-African initiative, when she worked as the Chair of the African Union-African Diaspora Health Initiative (AU-ADHI), since 2012. This organization mainly works to mobilize African health professionals in the Diaspora health professionals in assisting with Africa's continental healthcare crisis. Her Pan-African assignment also includes the African Union-Diaspora African Forum Americas (AU-DAF), an organization that she has been chairing since 2010. Most West Africans became familiar with the diplomat's impressive abilities and boldness when she launched the "Wakanda One Village Project" in January 2019. That project amazed many Africans because its objective was the real epitome of the Pan-African ideal. The Wakanda project (as it is generally referred to) was planning to build an extremely efficient "development infrastructure" which was to be, precisely, the following structure, in an African country: an ultramodern and efficient health facility, school, university, and all that a community needs to live in prosperous conditions. Africans in the Diaspora were willing and ready to be the complete force behind the project.

The Wakanda Project led Ambassador Arikana to visit Ghana in December 2021 with a group of black diasporans to sell the project. Ghanaians were enthusiastic and eager to see the project materialize. In their mind, such an infrastructure would once again echo the strategic and preferred location of their country for Pan-African achievements. But other Ghanaians were afraid of a situation that would lead to parochial individual petty interests being given preeminence over the multitude's benefit that the Wakanda project represents. Some months down the line it was rumored that Ghana did not win the position of the "seat" of the project, and that a southern African country or several of them had obtained that privilege and sadly enough, the reason that most citizens heard was that the demand for little bribes disappointed the mental and physical architects of the mega-project. During that meeting, that was held in one of the most prestigious hotels of Cape Coast in the Central Region of Ghana, the audience witnessed for the first time the bold, innovative, and constructive ideas of Ambassador Arikana.

The choice of Ghana for this project could be related to the prominent presence of Pan-Africanism at the core of early postcolonial Ghana's policy and politics, with President Kwame Nkrumah. Ambassador Arikana was championing such gigantic visionary activities, although she was no longer the ambassador of the African Union (AU) to the US.

The message of this ambassador has struck over and over again these flails: colonialism, neo-colonialism, imperialism, injustice, and similar phenomena or rapacious deeds of the Western countries in their interactions or "collaborations" with Africa. She relates most of these calamities to the 1885 Berlin Conference. It therefore did not come as a surprise when, in October 2019, the ambassador was removed from her position as representative of the African Union (AU) to Washington. Her open, vitriolic, radical, and Fanonist position could not be tolerated for long by Western institutions.

As part of her Pan-Africanist mission, Ms. Arikana was in Burkina Faso in 2024, with a group of Black Diasporans whom she introduced to the Burkinabè president Captain Ibrahim as "sons and daughters" of Africa who were, in most cases traveling back to Africa for the first time, and she asserted her alliance and acceptance of the political line that Burkina Faso had decided to embark on. Ambassador Arikana, as she is always called, bought into the anti-imperialist policy of the Burkinabè regime and does not hesitate to mention the Burkinabè decision as an example to be emulated by the whole of Africa. Dressed in a red T-shirt and a red beret, the accoutrement of a true freedom fighter, she commended the Burkinabè president as a visionary reincarnation of revolutionary

Thomas Sankara, and applauded the young president's determination to implement the core message behind the creation of the Organization of the African Unity (OAU) in 1963. Let us remember that the OAU is the predecessor of the African Union, AU. In a speech at the University of Cape Coast on August 21, she said, "We need more Traorés in Africa", an expression that poses her admiration of the blunt de-linking anti-imperialist policy (and many of its components) that the country of the incorruptible Man embarked upon.

That 2-day lecture was indeed the 14th Kwame Nkrumah Memorial Lecture, an event that is regularly held and confers doctorate degrees on prominent figures, who are most of the time political figures and distinguished academics. Several African presidents and black scholars were conferred degrees by the University of Cape Coast in line with the practice of the Kwame Nkrumah Memorial Lecture. South African Thabo Mbeki and Professor Emmanuel Kwaku Akyeampong Ellen Gurney, Professor of History and of African-American Studies at Harvard University in the US, were the speakers of the 13th Memorial held in 2023. This week, Ambassador Arikana "graced" the University of Cape Coast with lectures on the theme "imperialism, colonialism and neo-colonialism, the three axes of evil for Africa". These lectures once again revealed the courageous, outspoken, and liberatory attitude and spirit of the diplomat. The audience could notice that some of the ambassador's statements were overt indictments of some Ghanaians. She plainly believes her generation (regardless of their location in Africa), who belong to the generation of postcolonial African cadres, civil servants, and decision makers, has failed the African youth.

Other exciting ideas in her lecture were the hope that the African youth represents and the power that lies in the hands of African women. To the youth, she said, "If your president, your minister, does not work towards the defense of the interests and the progressive move of your society, remove him or her." To women, she had this to say: "Men owe us, women, because we gave birth to them; we must therefore have mutual respect and harmony. But if the men refuse that you sit at the dinner table with them, take that chair and get yourself a seat. If the men in your country coil in their shell and are incapable of condemning the corruption that retards the development of your country, take that role/job upon yourselves". These examples certainly remind the listener and reader of the following occurrences: the removal of dictator Blaise Compaoré from power in Burkina Faso in 2014 by young men and women, certain moments and august persons that make the pride of Africa like Yaa Asantewaa and the amazons in general, and the historical protest of women who devised an impeccable strategy and walked hundreds of miles to defy the French colonial police in Mali and Senegal, when the men were beaten to submission.

Ambassador Arikana's whole trajectory as a diplomat and an activist represents one of courage, determination, passion, vision, and exemplary leadership. Her tours, lectures, and speeches unequivocally attack and condemn the human and material hindrances to the onward march of Africa and her diaspora. What most of her listeners wish now is the implementation of her ideas and statements. Since she was speaking in university whose primary mandate is the training of teachers in Ghana, Ambassador Arikana recommended that the teaching of Kwame Nkrumah's writings be made compulsory at the University of Cape Coast (and certainly other universities in the country), and she recommended, for a better understanding of the machinery of imperialism the following book: *Confessions of an Economic Hitman* by John Perkins.

PART III

PART 3: ARTS, ENVIRONMENT, EDUCATION, AND CULTURE

THE FANTASY COFFINS OF GHANA: HIDDEN COMPETITORS IN WORLD ARTISTRY

Ideas, beliefs, and considerations behind death vary from community to community, all across the world. The general belief is that while the dead are considered to be "gone" as it is believed in general in the West, the dead live with those alive in Africa and other non-Western areas. While life is generally seen as linear in the Western worldview, we have a cyclical consideration of life and death in Africa and other areas. Several writers put it implicitly or explicitly that the dead continue their activities when they transition to the other world. In Yoruba mythology and several African cultures, the dead have to be buried with their servants, and such a practice is considered a normal act. In Ghana, this belief and practice are manifested in a slightly different, artistic, and creative way. The fantasy coffin makers showcase that continuity between life and death, and go beyond that. The art started in the Ga community along the coast in Accra, Ghana. Coffins translate or convey the profession, trade, or habit of the deceased through exquisite relevant motifs.

That accounts for the array of coffins displayed by the seaside, on the coast, where the Ga community resides. Eric Anang, a coffin maker, explains how this came to be when he traces the practice to the Kings' palanquins in History, with their shapes and designs: spider for some, cocoa for others, etc. With time, the ordinary citizen has access to that luxury, and people come to him to immortalize or celebrate someone who is no more. The family members mention or explain the occupation or favorite activity of the dead relative, and ask the artist to make a coffin that captures exactly those, and the intention behind the whole practice is to allow, or ensure that the "departed one" who simply transitioned into that other realm will continue their trade or habit there. So artists like Eric and his trainees make coffins which have the following shapes, among others: a vegetable like pepper when the dead was a farmer, the coffin has the shape, colors and inscriptions on a Ghana Airways aircraft when the deceased was a pilot, guns for soldiers or hunters, a canoe or fish for fisher-folks, light bulbs for electricians and a little bit of humor crips into reality when the coffin has the shape of cigarette pack, a phallus, or wee joint. These are said to reflect, respectively, the situation of a deceased who was a heavy smoker, a "womanizer," a term in Ghana somehow synonymous with "Don Juan," and the joint would be made for a wee smoker. So the motif conveys the person's identity, celebrates their life, and ensures the continuity of the person's life in the other world.

In most cases, the coffin is shown to the family members on Thursday in communities like Teshie (in Accra), on Friday, which is wake keeping, the body is taken from the mortuary and displayed in the coffin, and on Saturday, the burial takes place. In certain cases, with the fast pace of life, the bereaved family gets to see the coffin only on Saturday, and scuffles ensue when the family is not exactly satisfied with the design of the coffin, but such arguments are quickly settled.

The coffin makers do not always have it easy since they are despised by some members of the community, they are often looked down upon and branded as "people who call death," so that they can make good business, or "merchants of death. Therefore, when artists try to display their beautiful artworks in popular galleries and other spaces where they can be noticed, they encounter some hostility. Many believe that coffin makers perform libations so that more people die and the sale of coffins booms. A coffin maker explains how he was forced to withdraw his artwork, which he displayed in Accra around 37 Military Hospital and the Airport area, which are popular spots, to advertise his work and skills. To his surprise, the city authorities forced him to take the coffins away because he was bringing death into the community. The coffin maker or carpenter is therefore often called *"gunyoadeka,"* which means "coffin" in Ga (the community along the coast in Accra). Fortunately, institutions like Alliance Française and the Goethe Institute encourage the display of such works of art, and several Ghanaians patronize such exhibitions and learn more since some of them do not know that this combination of artwork and celebration of life exists in their own county or city.

Practically, this is how the artist works: coffins are made from fresh wood, since that is more affordable to the artists, and numerous pieces of wood are joined in a crafty manner, plus three coats of "sanding and painting" (sometimes five) in order to get rid of traces of joints and increase the aesthetics. Satin and foam are displayed inside the coffin in order to absorb liquid, since the body is retrieved from the mortuary and laid inside the coffin, based on the requirements of the various ceremonies, which themselves reflect the customs of the areas. The artists also learn from the communities they meet during their trips and exhibitions: while they use gasoline (as a solvent), oil-based (enamel) paint in Ghana, in Europe, and

America, they picked up the habit of using acrylic, which is less harmful to human health.

A slight variety shows how trenchant the creativity and imagination of these artists is: they do not limit their work to Accra, they take it to other cities like Kumasi, in Ghana and to Europe and the USA (as mentioned above) and in the West they are referred to as 'artists' not 'coffin makers or carpenters', as one of them jokingly points out; that broadens the minds of their audience or viewers, in the West. In Kumasi, the art takes a different form: instead of making coffins after orders have been placed by customers or relatives of the deceased, in Kumasi, the artists are more interested in listening to the stories on the communities and the stories of people's lives; based on that, coffins are made to celebrate such lives and sometimes, artworks are hatched to celebrate events, and such art works are displayed in shops or galleries; unlike Teshie (Accra) where the artist is limited in the choices and compelled to sticks to the demands of the customers, in Kumasi the artist has more freedom and adds more fun and imagination to their work.

Fantasy coffins are not always made to celebrate life; they also convey a message. The artist can make a coffin in the form of a gun, which is broken into two pieces in the presence of people, as a way of saying that it is time to put an end to gun violence. Mr. Anang did such work during a residency at UW-Madison, in support of the Black Lives Matter movement, and it was a success, a real way of putting the life of the community (where he finds himself) at the center of his art. The same artists also show how eco-conscious they are when they craft coffins in the shape of fireflies or honeybees.

The artists move their story (ies) and do not remain fixed in time and space; they broaden the function and story of the coffin.

This ingenuity deserves more attention. So much knowledge lies behind these coffins, and it should not come as a surprise if, in some years to come, one sees them in a competition with the chefs-d'oeuvre of Pablo Picasso, Leonardo da Vinci, and others.

SETTING THE RECORD STRAIGHT: WORLD CIVILIZATION STARTED IN AFRICA

Manicheist views do not help in anyway. They simply apportion blames, and strive to identify or pinpoint what any specific institution or individual is responsible of. 'World civilization, Africa and Europe' is a theme that generated much writing. Afrocentric/Africentric scholars have demonstrated the contribution of Africa to world civilization. Cheikh Anta Diop in the African Origin of Civilization: Myth or Reality (1974) and the writings of his close friend from Congo Theophile Obenga, posit, calmly and unemotionally the pivotal contribution of Africa to world civilization. Diop uses carbone-14 dating (a scientific method that can accurately determine the age of organic materials as old as approximately 60,000 years) and linguistic studies that scientifically conclude that subjects like Geometry, Mathematics, Rhetoric, etc, were present in Africa when Europe had no knowledge of these subjects. These radical and ground breaking conclusions could not be accepted when Europeans and when Cheikh Anta Diop was searching for a university where he could enroll and conduct studies along those lines. He was denied admission and only one of the French Universities accepted him, on condition that he removes certain portions from his research, and those were the most instrumental in negating the Eurocentric domination in world civilization. Diop certainly agreed to compromise to some extent, but the core of his thesis remained intact.

Antimanicheism is recommended here because I am of the view that the role of Africa in world civilization or the gigantic contribution of Africa to world civilization has to be pointed out, in other words, Africa must be given her fair place or contribution in world civilization and then we move on. In other words, I believe that unveiling the contribution of Africa to word civilization should not generate any conflict or misunderstanding. All that needs to be done is to show that world civilization started in Africa and then we move on to other pressing issues. That comes to the point of 'the blame game has to end', which means 'stating once and for all the fact that Greece learned what she boasts of from Africa'. Greek scholars travelled to Africa to learn from African scholars and reversed the course of history by falsifying things and writing that Greece brought civilization to the world. Adopting such an attitude would simply mean setting the record straight by giving Africa what she deserves, and then the regular or daily activities of every society go on. It would not help in any way to spend much time or engage in bitter fights on that issue. A contemporary scholar who contributes in an efficient manner to the education of African children or the black youth on the fundamental values, activities, scholarship and discoveries that drive today's world is Dr. Philemon MOUKEBE from Cameroon in his video sessions whose length and content are simply appropriate. He teaches using a simple and appropriate pedagogy. Some of the most important contributions that Africa brought to world civilization and that are likely to remain hidden from the African or black youth and children are revisited by Dr. MOUKEBE. I will touch upon some of those Africa institutions and studies that sustain today's society. Through the *Afrique Avenir*

(Afrofuturism) Foundation most of those contributions of Africa are unveiled.

So, these are points whose inclusion in the curriculum of black students or any world civilization course would open the learners 'eyes to some events that moulded global civilization, from an open-minded and non-biased stance. In Western Universities, especially in the US, the current tendency is to host Arts and Sciences under the same umbrella, in the same college as a result, American universities have Colleges of Arts and Sciences. This certainly denotes the connection between these 2 areas of study which might seem to be different. Joining them is a laudable scholarly gesture and stressing the nexus between Arts and Sciences was present in African learning institutions 77,000 years before Christ (BC). In Blombos Cave, an archaeological site located in Blombos Private Nature Reserve, about 300 km east of Cape Town on the Southern Cape coastline in South Africa, geometric rules and applications were written on rocks. The most informative archaeological material from Blombos Cave includes engraved ochre, engraved bone ochre processing kits, terrestrial and marine faunal remains. That revealed how human-related activities could co-exist with those of the sciences or those that require more investigation and research, or are less overt. This cave produced a paradigm shift in the understanding of the timing and location of the development of modern human behavior. No sign of geometry existed in the world before the excavation of Blombos Cave. Reputed historians have it that geometry started in Africa, based on that cave. Still in the area of Mathematics, another important element is the Ishango Bone, which is the proof that Africans were familiar with calculus 22,000 years

BC and let us remain mindful of the fact that Africans have been living on the continent for 300,000 years. The Ishango Bone which was discovered at the "Fisherman Settlement" of Ishango in the Democratic Republic of Congo is a bone tool and possible mathematical device.

Regarding the Empires, we are bound to pay special attention to Imhotep, a black man from Egypt also known as the "Father of Medicine". In 2,700 BC, he wrote a treaty of medicine, and the Greek Hippocrates studied that treaty in 500 BC, in Alexandria in Egypt. So Imhotep preceded Hippocrates in the field of medicine, 2,200 years. Hippocrates is therefore not the inventor of Medicine but rather Imhotep the African. The latter was ultimately turned into a god by Hippocrates. So the Hippocratic Oath (the ethics guiding the practice of medicine) which is taken by medical students who are about to start practicing is in reality not an oath taken to Hippocrates, but rather to Imhotep, the teacher of Hippocrates, the Greek. Hippocrates learned so much from the African Imhotep that he deified the later, he turned Imhotep a god: Asclepius, the Greek god that physicians take the oath to. So the Hippocratic Oath is in reality an oath taken to the African Imhotep or the god he incarnates, Asclepius. Imhotep went further and developed the rules of modern architecture and trained several architects like Senemout, also an African, who built the first house with 2 floors, Queen Hatshepsout' s palace, 1,500 years BC. It is generally referred to as "the finest example of the brilliant architecture that once existed during the days of ancient Egypt." It might help to know that what is taught in schools today as the theorems of Pythagoras and Thales are Egyptian theorems, conceived during the construction of the pyramids, 1,500 years in Egypt before Pythagoras and Thales were born. So, Pythagoras theorem is therefore not the theorem invented by Pythagoras, but rather a sample of African knowledge. The original copy of that theorem is currently on a papyrus in the British Museum in England.

Modern writing was also born in Egypt and was called 'the word of God' which later was called hieroglyphics or sacred graphics by the Greeks. The writing was done on papyrus, which is the first version of paper as we know it today, so paper was invented in Africa. The papyrus were compiled into the 'Biblos' by the Greeks and the location of the books was therefore called 'bibliothèque' or library, and 'biblos' will also provide the word 'Bible', the word of God. The first library in the world was therefore erected in Africa, that of Alexandria in Egypt, around the 3rd century BC. Paper and writing started there so they had to be preserved. Greek writing and Latin writing as well as Greek numbers therefore have an African origin. The Egyptians produced 3 different alphabets out of the hieroglyphics and 2 of them are the hieratic and demotic. It is today possible to write all the languages in the world because of those 3 alphabets.

FIRST PAN-AFRICAN WOMEN'S CONFERENCE AND ITS RELEVANCE: GHANA 1960 REMAINS A GIANT

Pan-Africanism has brought together continental Africans and Black Diasporans several times. While the first idea that comes to many people in Africa is Kwame Nkrumah efforts towards uniting all African nations, a task he mentioned over and over again, all his life both as President in Ghana and as co-president in Guinea after he was overthrown, another meaning of Pan-Africanism is the relations between blacks on the African continent and blacks in the diaspora (often called Black diasporans) who reside mostly in the north America (US and Canada), South America and the Caribbean. The coincidence is that Nkrumah was the driving force behind all these 2 understandings or definitions of Pan-Africanism. Be it the union or unity of all African nations or the relations between continental Africans and Black diasporans, the Ghanaian first leader could not be excluded from the debate. In 1960, barely 3 years after the Gold Coast became independent and renamed Ghana, Accra hosted one of the most iconic events in the life of black women in the world: the Conference of Women of Africa and African Descent (CWAAD) which took place in July 1960. The conference was held at the University College of Ghana, today's University of Ghana, Legon, and it certainly was a high point in transnational solidarity efforts among Black women who then attempted to lay out the terms, implications, necessity and importance of their transnational relationships. This conference underscores 2 important global movements or phenomena which can be put, succinctly and in simple terms, this way: Pan-Africanism and Feminism, or Pan-

African Feminism, or Black Feminism which has come to represent Womanism, a literary trend or movement founded by Alice Walker, and captures the realities of African and African American Women, which Alice Walker and many find to be different from Feminism, which to them conveys more the conditions of white women.

This first conference is of vital importance since it demonstrates the foresightedness of Kwame Nkrumah who took the first step in a process that will ultimately develop and grow ramifications of various sorts: At the global level, the Accra 1960 Conference of Women of Africa and African Descent came to be before the International Women's Day which burgeoned in 1910 as an International Conference of Working Women after the German communist activist and advocate of women's rights Clara Zetkin put forth the idea in Copenhagen. It took more than 60 years for the UN to approve the Women's International Day in 1975 as a holiday celebrated on March 8th. The Accra event is therefore older than the current International one and the goals of the former were more specific and fit extremely well the then prevailing context which was the anticolonial struggles across the world and the golden age Black Nationalism, the Civil Rights Movement and the prevalence of Third-Worldism; Gamal Abdel Nasser of Egypt, Ahmed Sukarno of Indonesia and Jawaharlal Nehru of India were the leaders and brains behind the last one. The pointed and focused nature of the 1960 Accra women's conference is captured in these 3 points: (a) to promote leadership and citizenship amongst women of Africa and African descent; (b) to give the opportunity to discuss their common problems and how best these could be solved; (c) to promote friendship amongst women of Africa and African descent. It therefore celebrated women's contribution to the liberation struggles, and also created a platform to reflect over the role of black women in a free socialist and united Africa that has a harmonious relationship with the black diaspora. The revolutionary role of women was stressed, and the link between the total liberation of Africa and the complete emancipation of African women was voiced. One could see that last point to be prophetic, if we try to answer the question whether the total liberation of Africa has been achieved. I am of the view that it has not been achieved yet.

The Ghana Organization of Women already existed, with strong members like Hannah Cudjoe, a prominent activist for Ghanaian independence in the 1940s and 50s and propaganda secretary of the Convention People's Party (CPP), Nkrumah's party. Mrs. Cudjoe and the Ghana Women's Organization were the main architects of that first diasporic women's conference. Other prominent Ghanaian women with a political inclination at that time were Dr. Evelyn Amarteifio, Letitia Quaye, Miss Sophia Doku, Grace Ayensu and several others. Many of them were MPs, a decision which reflects the pivotal role that Kwame Nkrumah assigned to women in the sociopolitical life of every society in general and Ghana in particular. The conference spelled clearly both a political agenda and a gender-related one, in Nkrumah's opening speech; they are respectively the following: the non-aligned neutrality in the Cold War with Ghanaian leadership of Pan-Africanism, and the fact that that men alone cannot eliminate the artificial boundaries which separate brother from brother and sister from sister on the continent and between the continent and the Americas and the Caribbean. The American delegation had among others the following prominent personalities and civil rights activists: Shirley Graham DuBois, Dorothy Ferebee, Anna Arnold Hedgeman and Pauli Murray. Several years later, other organizations emerged to defend women's rights like the Pan-African Women's Organization (PAWO) which is also the Specialized Agency of the African Union (AU) dedicated to gender equality and women's empowerment; PAWO is celebrated on 31st July every year. The African Renaissance and Diaspora Network (ARDN) is a more recent organization concerned among others with issues confronting black women on the continent and the diaspora. Ghana and Nkrumah once again assert their position as the pioneer of an all-inclusive and gender- conscious Pan-Africanism.

BURKINA FASO AT LOGGERHEADS WITH BBC, VOA AND HUMAN RIGHTS WATCH

News circulating during the first trimester of 2024 had it that the Burkinabè transitional government and certain media and international institutions were in a silent but bellicose confrontation. The British Broadcasting Corporation (BBC), Voice of America (VOA) and Human Rights International suddenly had suddenly fallen out of the good graces of the junta in power. The reasons for this fracas are the military forces of Burkina being accused of the mass killing of civilians.

This kind of contention does not come as a surprise in a country where war against terrorists is lasting, and exhausting everybody and the only factor that keeps people going and fighting is the determination, power of conviction and persuasion of the government in power. Once in a while one could hear civilians talking of the "burden" of the financial contribution they are making as "war effort" but in reality, the majority of citizens strongly believe that the transitional government is performing well, in this combat against terrorists. It might help to remind readers that the perseverance of the terrorists' attacks caused the overthrow of 2 regimes that lost their credibility and capability in the eyes of the Burkinabè: the presidency of Roch Marc Christian Kaboré and that of Lieutenant Colonel Damiba.

The cliché goes that one cannot make omelet without "breaking" eggs, which in other words means that no grand measure or action can be undertaken by a government without causing any collateral damage or casualties. Some innocent victims will always emerge. The same criticism was raised against several political regimes that ultimately went down in History as good leaders.

In the same country, Thomas Sankara was accused of the violation of human rights when a group of officers belonging to the so called "old obstacle to the young revolution" were shot in 1983. Then, when a large number of basic education teachers went on strike in 1984, they were terminated for their action. Once again, Sankara was blamed but posterity got to know, that the second in command at that time, former President Blaise Compaoré was behind that decision to fire workers who simply applied their right to aspire to better working conditions. Those who knew Sankara well would agree that he strongly believed in the power of argumentation and supported trade unions which he was always ready to discuss with, although once in a while he would issue threats to the most radical ones. But definitely, to fire basic education workers for embarking upon a strike action does not fit the leftist and Marxist ideology espoused by Sankara. But the whole criticism is understandable and necessary in such a context. Speculations and opinions should be allowed to fly, freely. To criticize Sankara is therefore a normal thing, in a context of "democratic centralism", as Sankara himself used to call his governance model. And that measure had a very negative impact on education in Burkina. A vertiginous decline was noticed in students' levels since the time those seasoned teachers were fired and replaced with new and young ones who were about to complete their training. In a nutshell, many people are strongly convinced that Sankara and the 1983 revolution was wrongly accused for that decision which to many Burkinabè and other nationals was a "very wicked" one.

Another occurrence that might contribute to tarnish the reputation to some extent of this current transitional government in Burkina is the unlawful activities that some Volunteers for the Defense of the People (VDP) are often accused of. One often sees on social media some members of that unit, being presented as robbers who used their weapons to steal from populations instead of protecting them, in the anti-terrorist war. The veracity of these allegations is to be checked.

The most recent accusation against the Burkinabè anti-terrorist forces is dubbed a "massacre" of innocent civilians that occurred on February 25, 2024 in Soro and Nodin, 2 villages in the Western north region of the country. The press reports that 220 lives were lost, and 56 of the victims were children. Africa News in its publication of March 22, 2024 writes that "more than 220 civilians, among them at least 56 children fell victim to atrocities allegedly committed by the country's military... These mass killings are some of the most egregious abuses by the army in nearly ten years". Details on the incident posit that 100 soldiers descended on the civilians in those localities, "shortly after some Islamist fighters had passed the area". The soldiers then gathered the population and mercilessly opened fire on them, no one was spared. The same news agency adds that the soldiers repeated their brutal and cruel action by shooting indiscriminately at residents and the reason for the killing remains the same: Islamist fighters passing through the area and (probably) striking and alliance with them against the national troops.

It is not a secret that in the understanding of the general public, Islamist fighters are the enemies, those opposing the national armed forces who are fighting to secure the national territory, the populations and fighting for the return of calm and normalcy in Burkina; the country has been woefully shaken and deteriorated by this war. The debate revolved around the connection between the "enemies" or terrorists and Islamists. Scholars in Islam and defenders of peaceful coexistence devoted ample time and effort, explaining that the forces facing the national army and volunteer fighters are terrorists and not Islamists. Others pointed out clearly that referring to the terrorist as "jihadists" was not appropriate. The reality on the ground seems to be that almost all terrorists gunned down by the Burkinabè defense forces are either Fulani (the nomad cattle breeders), or people who have some link with the Fulani and that accounts for these cattle breeders being pinpointed as terrorists. Sources contend that the majority of the Fulani had to leave the Burkinabè territory and seek refuge in neighboring Côte d'Ivoire among others, for their own safety. They believe that Burkinabè soldiers shoot them because they are seen to be terrorists.

A video that circulated on social media shows armed Muslims delivering a message to the Burkinabè president Captain Ibrahim Traoré and his government; the essence of the message was that an Islamic force or campaign is aiming at defeating the regime and turning Burkina Faso, Niger and Mali into Islamic nations where the Sharia law is the nerve of governance. If the authenticity of that video is established, one could understand partly why the armed forced or soldiers and volunteer fighters would perceive the current war as a war against Islamist fighters. But what is obvious is that nothing explains and defends the killing of more than 200 civilians, because Islamist combatants passed through their locality. If indeed, that action of the Islamists was verified and proved to be true, investigations had to be conducted, and culprits or the pro-Islamists (if such persons were identified) could be treated as the laws of the country stipulate. One could also attribute this mass killing, to the tension, fatigue and weariness of armed forces who have been fighting for years against "unknown" or "unidentified" enemies.

The fracas with the above-mentioned news agencies and the Human Rights Watch has to do with the coverage of that "mass killing" of civilians by the international media, including the Associated Press. The BBC and Voice of America (VOA) are certainly some of those international media. The statement issued by the Burkinabè national authorities last March is that "both radio stations (BBC and VOA) would be suspended for two weeks; they also warned other media networks to avoid reporting on the story. While the BBC did not respond to a request for comments, the VOA stands by its reportage on this event and goes further to state that it intends to continue to fully and fairly cover activities in the country (Burkina Faso)" according to Africa News Agency. This bourgeoning contention deserves a careful monitoring since it has the potential to "produce" other enemies to the Burkinabè politics and policy of the government.

THE CONFUSION BETWEEN CHILD LABOR AND EDUCATION IN AFRICA

According to UNICEF, the activities "given to children between 5 to 11 years of age are considered child labor if they work at least 28 hours a week".

There is a real thin line between child labor and education in Africa. The above sentence is the definition of child labor, according to UNICEF, the institution whose duty is to ensure the well-being of children all over the world. I find these definitions and classifications to be problematic. Geographical, social and cultural differences or realities have to be taken into consideration. I initially wrote a piece in which I pinpointed a confusion in the definition of another UNICEF- related preoccupation, the notion and 'child soldier'. The international texts say the following: 'child soldier refers to any boy or girl under age 18 who is recruited or used by an armed force or armed group in any capacity. It does not refer only to a child who is taking a direct part in hostilities. This second statement about child soldiers is in contrast with the previous one: 'Children who have not attained the age of fifteen years shall neither be recruited in the armed forces or groups nor allowed to take part in hostilities.'

In other words, per this statement, age 15 is the key criterion in the definition or consideration of child soldier, while the previous one mentions age 18 years. This obviously shows that the rules and regulations on which the whole world relies on are not quite coherent and need revision, overhauling or clarity to attract more trust and reliability. But the focus of this piece is the concept of child labor. If we take into consideration the practice and requirements of education in several societies, especially in Africa, what is branded as 'child labor' is often confidently seen and considered as part and parcel of education. The illustration of the nebulousness that surrounds the notion of child labor in Africa is noticed when some adults reminisce their youthful days, when they were around 15 or 14 and carrying hoes, posing for a picture, on their way to or from the farm. A professor who looked at one of such pictures wrote "I miss those year. That was not child labor at all". Strangely enough, all the reactions that I gathered, and that refute the blanket definition of child labor come from educationalists, professors and coincidentally the comments were passed on May Day or Workers' Day. Some years ago, one of them said "our parents were not very rich civil servants, they were overage level employees, and we joyously assisted them in any way we could, on the farm. So, the notion of child labor is relative" she concluded. In communities where cattle's breeding is the main activity, like the Fulani in West Africa, the duty of a young boy who reaches age 11 is to look after the cattle of the family and see to it that they graze among other things. Various techniques are taught to them, like how to ensure control over the cattle, where the best pastures and water points are, when to take the animals to the pastures, etc. The cattle are the sole and main property and source of livelihood for the Fulani families. Therefore, taking care of animals is fundamental in the upbringing of boys.

Raising a child in such societies is an activity that is based on pragmatism, acquiring skills required by the community. As a result, girls also are taught very early how to carry out chores required from them. Sexism has been eradicated in most societies today so a task like cooking is taught to both young males and females. Boys are told that learning and knowing culinary activities makes them autonomous and independent in life. In communities where washing machines are non-existent, boys and girls are taught how to launder with their hands, and as a result, it is common to see a couple doing the household laundry together: the man washes the clothes and his wife rinses them and the man might then dry them in the sun. This is a repartition of tasks which I do not call division of labor since this is no labor but rather a compulsory and deliberate work in the family. Many children as young as 7 years, especially girls begin to learn how to wash their own clothing, starting from the lightest ones and their parents (mothers most of the time) wash the slightly heavier ones, while the girls watch and learn. That guarantees that the young girl will grow into a woman who can launder for her family (while teaching her ward[s] the same activity).

This is such an important education because in rural Africa and the average African city, washing machines are not that common and a woman who cannot launder brings embarrassment onto herself. The same applies with cooking meals. A lady who is incapable of cooking meals for her family might lose her marriage, since her husband can send her to her parents, for them to teach her how to cook. Per the definition or criterion presented by UNICEF (the one I opened this piece with), an 11-year-old Fulani boy who attends school and takes the cattle to graze 2 hours in the morning before he goes to school and 2 hours after school, from Monday to Friday and does the same thing 4 hours over the weekend (Saturday and Sunday) would clock 28 hours, tending to the family cattle. That fulfills all the requirements of child labor while the young man is rather lending a helping hand to the family, to guarantee and protect the source of income of the household. At the same time, the boy is acquiring the skills required of him, as a man who belongs to a "tribe" of cattle breeders. If he grows up into a man who cannot tend to those animals, he might not find it easy making money, since that task is their main activity. The person might be gainfully employed in an institution but rearing cattle on the side will provide extra income. The young 10-year-old girl who spends about 3 hours every day by her mother's side learning recipes and other culinary practices is simply edifying herself into a respectable skilled woman in society. She is not entangled in forced labor in any way. The main point I am making is that sharing tasks with one's parents trains the young ones and prepares them for the main activities society expects from them.

We should not lose sight of the fact that child labor really exists in the world, sadly enough and of course in Africa. Wealthy farmers who seek cheap labor contract the services of young boys and girls, below the age of 15, to work on their farm, for long hours. Migration from rural areas to the city in search of greener pastures forces young boys and girls into extremely tedious and hazardous activities.

A case in point is the plight of the penniless girls from Northern Ghana who travel to the southern cities, especially to Accra where they really toil. They live on coins gathered by carrying heavy loads of merchandise bought by customers, in the market. They live in squalor, in open areas, vulnerable and they are called the "Kaya Girls". Their aim in most cases is to "make enough money" to buy a sewing machine and return to their native communities and start a job, sewing. The boys and girls who are forced to drop out of school or who simply stay out of school and work on cocoa farms in Ghana are trapped in forced labor. The simple fact to imagine those youngsters who are the hands behind the production of cocoa that is ultimately processed into chocolate takes away one's appetite for chocolate. The fishing sector in Ghana relies a lot on child labor (tragically, many of the children end up dead) and gold mining activities involve the same exploitation. Child labor is therefore a reality and should not be condoned under any circumstance. But let us avoid the serious mistake of taking societal organic training of youngsters to be child labor. That is an indictment of noble and compulsory training which is hundred per cent beneficial to children and the whole community. The difference must be made clear, and the UN texts should not be contradictory.

STUDENTS' ACCOMODATION ON AFRICAN UNIVERSITY CAMPUSES

The days when University students were sure to live in decent rooms seem to be long gone. Many still reminisce the times when porters at their halls of residence and employees at the university restaurant treated students with great respect. Some go the extent of stating that they were attending to by Western workers, in the restaurants. What all this says is the fact that living conditions on university campuses in most African countries have drastically deteriorated. This nosedive in the standards keeps worsening; it is reaching very worrisome levels.

Appalling Living Conditions on University Campuses in Ghana

Insalubrity is the common denominator. Hygiene is extremely poor, large numbers of students live in a single room, balconies are turned in to rooms, and storage space is hurriedly converted into rooms. Let's ponder the situation in 2 West African countries: the University of Cape Coast in Ghana, and the University of Lagos, Nsukka, Nigeria. The University of Cape Coast was established in 1962 with the main aim of training tutors. These are some of the halls of residence the University boasts of: Atlantic Hall (ATL), Adehye Hall, SRC Hall (which was built by the Student Representative Council) and Superannuation Hall (founded by a joint effort of lecturers' union and the public sector). The first 2 are public, while the last 2 are semi- public, since non -public bodies have a share in them. In

Atlantic Hall, the regular scene is to have 5 students in a room. It is a mixed hall (with male and female students) and a room is not specious enough to accommodate 5 students. Adeheye Hall is solely for ladies, and a room which is to accommodate 2 or 3 ladies is crammed with 8. The same overcrowding applies to the other public halls of the University of Cape Coast: Valco, Casford, Oguaa halls. The semi-public halls are slightly better, numbers are lower in each room, but the "traditional halls" or the public ones that were built earlier do not present any good picture. It is disheartening to see young men and women struggling through such difficulties. Accommodation costs more than tuition and to top it all, security is very poor. Robberies are common due to many reasons: not enough security officers are employed; some of them are not trustworthy since no criminal background check is conducted as part of their recruitment process, etc.

The University of Nigeria, Nsukka

This institution is experiencing similar problems. Recently, students in the University of Nigeria, Nsukka, embarked on demonstrations because of the lack of accommodation. With over 40,000 students and a yearly intake of about 10,000, hostels in that university could barely accommodate one third of the students. One of the oldest halls of the institution, Nkurumah Hall (as it is called) had extremely deplorable conditions that were circulating on social media. Students had no steady power supply for three months and relied on generators and intermittent power supply; they complained that hostels stank because there was no water. For several months, students bemoaned the bad state of the hostels and to their utter surprise, the central administration sent staff from Works Department to remove every electrical installation from their rooms with a promise to renovate the rooms within some few weeks. Then nothing was done, resulting to the students' makeshift electrical installations.

Private Hostels: the Bad Semblance of Solution in Cape Coast

While this horrendous accommodation situation shakes campuses, individuals embark on a new kind of business, that of private hostels. A considerable number of lecturers and also other investors from all walks of life build hostels or private halls of residence, in the vicinity of the University, most of the time. Several reasons account for this: the response to the increasing number of students is to allow only first year students to reside on campus. For the subsequent 3 years, students reside outside campus so most of them seek accommodation in private hostels and that compounds problems for students and concerned University lecturers and administrators. Those hostels are overcrowded, sanitary conditions are not better in any way, costs are higher than they are in halls of residence on campus, and the owners of these hostels increase prices as they please. The cost of water and electricity is factored into the cost for accommodation, water supply is seriously unreliable, and so is electricity supply. While school fees gravitate around 1,000 Ghana cedis per year, accommodation costs 5,000 to 6,000Ghana cedis per year. Security is more precarious inside the hostel and on the way to the classroom on campus. Students are aggressed on a regular basis, especially when they take shortcuts roads. The only little joy stems from the relative comfort in the rooms in those private hostels in Cape Coast. Numbers are less (1 or 2 students in a room) and furniture is available when students move in (beds, wardrobe, desk(s). air condition in certain cases) and the "landlords" sometimes ensure constant water and electricity supply. It is common to hear that many of those landlords, owners or caretakers have no respect for students.

So the solution to the accommodation crisis is not private hostels, but an honest partnership between the public sector and unions like that of lecturers, a partnership that resulted in the superannuation hall which is a real improvement. The SRC Hall also which was erected by the agreement between student organizations and the university authorities is also a hall that provides better conditions to students. The solution in the case of the University of Cape Coast and the University of Nigeria Nsukka is obviously to make students' accommodation a priority which is preciously guarded by the Office of the Dean of Student Affairs. One of the concrete strategies could be building annexes to the traditional halls as it was done at the University of Ghana, Legon, in Accra.

General Economic Crisis

No country escapes the sudden resurgence of vertiginous increase in prices, in all spheres of life. The cost of living increased 2 or 3 times within 2 months in these 2 countries (Ghana and Nigeria) and no country in the world seems to escape the increased cost of living. The average person links that to the increase in the price of fuel, a phenomenon triggered or worsened by the Russian invasion of Ukraine and others. Education is a sector that bears the brunt of this crisis. School fees have increased; students find it difficult getting accommodation or even worse, feeding themselves. Many of my students say that while the instructor is teaching, their mind is on "where their next meal will come from". It is almost impossible for students to run photocopies or buy teaching manuals because they simply cannot afford and their parents cannot help. Moral values are debased, female students resort to other less enviable ways to make both ends meet and male students struggle in their own ways. The impact of this crisis is crippling all sectors and that of the education system is more vexatious. Can we expect anything good in the future when students cannot concentrate in class because they are hungry? Isn't it dangerous when instructors find it hard to make up-to-date lesson notes because they do not have the money to buy the most recent books in their area of expertise?

PAN-AFRICAN FILM FESTIVAL FESPACO HIGHLIGHTS INSECURITY AND CHRONICLES WOMEN'S ADROITNESS

One of the editions of the biennale took place from February 25 to March 4, 2023, a total of 170 entries were selected for the festival including 15 fiction featured films. The highest prize was the Golden Stallion Award, the Stallion of Yennenga (Etalon d'or de Yennenga) and an amount of around US $30,000. It was awarded to the fictional or documentary feature film judged to be the best in depicting African realities and that was the 28th edition. It was hosted in turbulent context, marked by bloody jihadist attacks that caused death, forced displacement of populations, loss of property and several military coups in the country. The wide scope of the jihadist phenomenon could be felt throughout this film festival of the Black world. FESPACO is branded as a Black festival because films by black directors are the majority and productions of white film makers are also allowed in the competition. Mali which is also affected by the Al-Qaeda jihadist fight was highly represented by its prime Minister, Choguel Kokalla Maiga who was also guest of honor. In his statement, Mr. Maiga stressed the correlation between peace and culture in these terms: "culture has an avant-garde role to play in the peace process"; that reechoed the central theme and some of the concerns at the heart of this year's edition (peace and culture) and the theme of the festival was "African Cinemas and Peace Cultures". The president of the organizing committee was the Burkinabè Fidele Aymar Tamini who struck a note of practicality or pragmatism and not empty words when he added that, that this theme of the culture of peace "must be an artistic framework and not only political because it affects everyone." In other words, the leader of organizing committee was stressing the paramount role that art in general and cinema in particular plays in molding the daily realities of people; peace and war can be ignited as well as quenched or avoided when art plays its role well and fully. So during this 28th edition, participants' concern focused on stimulating national unity and strengthening ties with other countries.

Another factor that makes this year's celebration special is women's life or fate in such a bellicose sub-regional context. It really is a pleasant surprise to notice that almost half of the fiction films this year were made by women, which is a real premier event. The Burkinabè director Apolline Traoré whose film *Sira* that won the prestigious consolation silver award puts jihadist violence in the spotlight as it deals with the story of a woman who has been kidnapped by terrorists and is struggling to survive. Ms. Traoré says that her movie was inspired by her own experience and the history of her country, Burkina, when she witnessed one of the biggest massacres in the country's history, the tragedy of Yirigou - in the north western part of the country- that occurred in January 2019 and ended with 210 people dead. In *Sira*, the heroine is Sira, a female nomad who is on her way to meet her groom with her family. However, the group is attacked mid-journey by Islamist terrorists and the men are murdered. Sira is molested and left stranded in the desert to face what she believes is certain death. But she is a fighter; she takes refuge in a cave and weaves her survival plan. She epitomizes resistance, the spirit of "never giving up". The director points out that through this heroine, she is doing something close to her heart, which is to portray women as strong characters, something she elaborates in with these words: "I simply have to give them [women] a voice. Most of the time, they are portrayed as victims: People show women in refugee camps who have lost their fathers or husbands. But it's these same women who protect their children, who have used dangerous escape routes to save them, women, in fact, who have demonstrated how to survive. It is precisely these women who play a major role in the fight against the jihadists in Africa. Beside all that, women have several special gifts, they pay more attention to details, so they make very talented filmmakers". The Bronze also went to a female director, Kenya's Angela Wamai for her chef d'oeuvre *Shimoni*. It was therefore common during this 28th edition to hear that African cinema has now freed itself from Western models, with women leading the way. In a sentence, the movie *Shimoni* "features Geoffrey, a teacher newly released from prison who renegotiates the confines of the physical world while forced to face his nightmare in the flesh" and the director describes the task of the female film maker this way: "We have the responsibility to ask difficult and uncomfortable questions. We have the responsibility to make people look and listen, no matter how much they don't want to. It is our responsibility to give people the images to look at and enable them to listen to voices they haven't heard before."

The 38-year-old Tunisian director Youssef Chebbi won the coveted Stallion of Yennenga award (the top prize) for his oeuvre *Ashkal*, a murder mystery movie. It centers on the investigation into the killing of a caretaker on a construction site in Carthage (a suburb of Tunis). To Youssef Chebbi, his film "borrows things from Tunisian reality but looks at them from another point of view". Among those elements of Tunisian reality in the movie, one notices the legends and narrative that emerged during the Jasmine Revolution – the 28-day civil resistance campaign that began in December 2010 with the self-immolation of 26-year-old street vendor Mohamed Bouazizi in Sidi Bouzid. The revolution culminated in the ouster of the then Tunisian President Zine El Abidine Ben Ali. Chebbi's short but loaded comment about his movie is: "For me, the image of immolation is highly iconic; it permeates Tunisian society. Only a few years ago we said that people who immolated themselves were martyrs and now we call them the killjoys of the transition to democracy. It shows there's been a drift".

That 28th edition of FESPACO is the proof that a new era has dawned in African cinema. The theme, determination, awardees, key dignitaries are chosen in a way that translates the realities of the moment. Film directors succeed in capturing all those parameters within a short space and time. The novel gender dimension amazes everyone, and the interludes paid special homage to the brave civilian volunteers who fight on the anti-jihadist battle front. That showcase of the engagement of what is generally and debatably called the 7th Art (after architecture, sculpture, painting, music, poetry and dance) must keep its onward march while re-inventing itself.

GEORGE PADMORE: A CARIBBEAN KEY ARTISAN OF AFRICA'S DECOLONIZATION

There are remarkable pan-Africanists in all parts of Africa and its Diaspora. They have my total esteem and admiration. In this book, West Africa is much referred to or made mention of because most of the data and information I have comes from that geographical area. What I do in this work is to provide a pointed and informed reading on a certain dimension or chapter of Pan-Africanism. Other studies of that type can be done, focusing on other specific areas. So, analyzing information from West Africa and the Black Diaspora in this book does not erode the pan-African dimension assigned to the book. It rather gingers researchers to broaden this type of research and I would like to point out that some reflections have been couched on paper, in that respect.

On 28th June 2011, a blue plaque was unveiled at Padmore's former address, 22 Cranleigh Street in the London Borough of Camden (inner London), in a ceremony attended by the High Commissioner of Trinidad & Tobago, the High Commissioner of Ghana, the Mayor of Camden, and others. The importance attached to the blue plaque translates the giant status of Padmore who was referred to, during that ceremony as one of the most influential thinkers of the 20th century, a patriot and defender of the Black cause who lived in Ghana and played a key role in the anti-colonial struggle after the World War II. A blue plaque is known to be a permanent sign installed in a public place in the United Kingdom and elsewhere to commemorate a link between that location and a famous person, event, or former building on the site, serving as a historical marker. The attribution of such a distinction to a Black Trinidadian who devoted his life to anti-colonial struggle can be regarded as the obviousness of the grandeur of George Padmore and this gesture can also be interpreted as Britain being haunted to some extent by its colonial past, and the respect that British imperialism and capitalism have developed over time for freedom fighters who were their enemies for decades. This blue plaque also represents the victory of Liberal or Leftist Great Britain, over their conservative capitalist counterparts. All this calls for more reflection in this era, when statues and monuments are being judged and given a fate. Those deemed to represent domination, suppression and injustice are destroyed. The ones that are preserved or kept represent the pride of nations. George Padmore has such a strong connection with Africa that his recognition as a giant certainly means a lot for Africans, especially Ghanaians, whose country was the abode of Padmore for several years.

Early Days

George Padmore is a well-known figure in Africa, especially in circles that have connections with anti-colonial, anti-imperialist and pan-African movements. He is known among both English speaking and French speaking people, although Anglophones find it easier to engage the ideas and achievements of Padmore. Among Anglophone countries, Ghana is one that can boast of the closeness that it had with George Padmore, who moved there in 1957 after the country attained independence. He then worked as advisor to Kwame Nkrumah, just like many other Black Diasporans who brought their contribution to the development of Ghana and the decolonization of West Africa and the ultimate unity of Africa. The (initially) African American W.E.B. DuBois, C. L R James from Trinidad and many others are mentioned any time this debate starts. DuBois took a step that mesmerized many observers: he renounced his US citizenship and naturalized as a Ghanaian until his death that same year. He was interred in Accra, the city that harbors the magnificent historical DuBois Center, where the best documents on issues related to the Black world and also development are, can be found.

Communism, Pan-Africanism and Padmore's Legacy in Ghana

George Padmore who was born on 28th June 1903 in Trinidad, then part of the British West Indies was baptized Malcolm Ivan Meredith Nurse at birth, and later took the pseudonym George Padmore, a pseudonym which itself is known to be the result of the compounding of the Christian name of his father-in-law, George Semper, and the surname of the friend who had been his best man, Errol Padmore. This makes many readers think that Padmore attached a special value to marriage or family life. His ties with Ghana are very strong, since his paternal great-grandfather was known to be an Asante warrior who was taken prisoner and sold into slavery at Barbados, where his grandfather, James Hubert Alfonso Nurse was born. His father was a local schoolmaster who had married a lady from Antigua, Anna Susanna Symister. George Padmore had most of his education in his native Trinidad, where he worked as a reporter once he graduated from High School. Padmore cherished so much his African roots that he instructed that his daughter be named Blyden-Cowart, in honor of the African nationalist Edward Blyden of Liberia. Padmore travelled to the US to further his education and during those years, he fell in love with Communism, through the Workers' Communist Party (CPUSA). As an energetic worker and prolific writer, he was so instrumental in the Communist Party in the US that he was taken to Moscow to deliver an important address to the Communist International in 1929. He remained a socialist who worked for African independence and Garan Kouyaté, also a Communist from Ségou (in today's Mali) living in France helped him to familiarize himself more with the condition of the African. In 1934 Padmore moved to London, where he became 'the center' of a community of writers dedicated to Pan-Africanism and African independence. His boyhood friend C. L. R. James, also from Trinidad, was already there, writing and publishing. Through that circle, Padmore, Ras Makonnen from British Guiana, and Jomo Kenyatta from Kenya developed a solid friendship. Kenyatta and Peter Abraham (from South Africa) became also ideologically inseparable.

Before World War II, C.L.R. James left for the United States, where he met Nkrumah and gave him a letter of introduction to Padmore. When Nkrumah arrived in London, Padmore met him and it was the start of a long alliance. Padmore was then organizing the 1945 Manchester Pan-African Congress, attended also by DuBois, the American organizer of earlier Pan-African conferences. The Manchester Conference helped set the agenda for decolonization in the post-war period. Padmore's alliance with Nkrumah held firm. When Nkrumah returned to the Gold Coast in 1947 to lead its independence movement, Padmore advised him in long detailed letters and also encouraged him to write an autobiography. Padmore ultimately accepted Nkrumah's invitation to move to Ghana and work as his advisor on African Affairs. Padmore died on 23 September 1959, aged 56 and after a funeral service at a London crematorium, his ashes were buried at Christiansborg Castle in Ghana on 4 October 1959. The George Padmore Research Library, in the neighborhood of Ridge, Accra, Ghana, is named after him. According to the Ghanaian London-based broadcaster Cameron Duodu, "Many of the statements and pamphlets, as well as the correspondences with which leaders of the British colonies in Africa combated the policies of the Colonial Office in London, were drafted at the dining table of Padmore's residence, at 22 Cranleigh Street; that was also the venue of the 5th Pan-African Conference that Padmore organized in Manchester in 1945". Other African countries have Padmore at heart: In Nairobi, Kenya, one finds George Padmore Road and George Padmore Lane. Padmore unequivocally epitomizes the international dimension of anticolonialism and Pan-Africanism.

GREETINGS IN AFRICA

Greeting is a cultural convention and in Africa, its verbal articulation is as important as the gestures that come with it. Those gestures or postures include the following: a bow, a military kind of salute, lying flat on the ground, a wave, a handshake, or an oral statement. These greeting postures are mostly determined by social variables such as gender, age, class/status etc. Among the Akan of Ghana, for instance, a young lady is expected to bow while greeting the elderly; the young man is as well expected to salute the elderly while greeting; adults in similar age bracket will rather shake hands, while the middle finger snaps the middle finger of the one you are "shaking". People are always greeted from right to left, always with the right hand. Among the Yoruba of Nigeria, the act of lying flat to greet adults and traditional leaders is common. Similarly, among the Frafra of northern Ghana, greeting can take the form of reverence, when someone greets a royal with these terms '*zugu be tondo*', which literally translates 'my head is on the ground', meaning 'you have my utmost respect and devotion, Chief'. These gestures and postures are manifestations of courtesy among Africans. These ways of greeting certainly have few similarities and many differences compared to habits in Western cultures. The value of greeting is generally completely different, in the West and the general importance of greetings in Western culture can, is captured this way by Wojtowicz (2021): "the role of greetings is neglected. People no longer greet each other properly because they are frequently in a hurry. When meeting a friend unexpectedly, one often only waves his or her hand or nods and goes about his or her business. In the Western culture people somehow tend to forget that a greeting is an expression of joy, attention and consideration in a proportionate way toward family members and friends. When meeting a stranger, westerners are aware that making the first good impression is particularly important, so they put effort into their appearance eventually forgetting that it is a greeting that is crucial in creating the first good impression and setting a positive tone for the consecutive conversation". If we add waving to the discussion, we realize that another chasm exists between most African habits and the western ones, since waiving with one's left hand is not a problem in most western cultures, meanwhile Africans in general take offence at that. Greetings have also been considered as speech acts that are uttered in certain situations for particular purposes. To scholars like Shih, Wei, & Gnisci (2010), greetings fall within the category of 'expressives' of illocutionary acts, seen as acts of politeness. In certain cases, greetings are not occasions for real conversation and in certain African cultures, the response to a greeting is a brief, polite and positive reply which is also a greeting to the first interlocutor. Everyone deserves to be greeted, people greet each other whenever they meet, and the same individuals may exchange greetings several times a day. People greet each other regardless of whether they know each other or not.

Among the Dioula or Jula (it belongs to the Mande language family) of West Africa for instance, a morning greeting could be the following:
a/ i ni sogoma (good morning)
M'baa / n'see, i sira here ra? (Good morning [said differently by a male and a female] did you sleep well?"

In this context greeting translates into showing interest in the 'peace' of the first one to greet, since the answer is to find out if that one had a good night. This greeting could end with blessing(s) for the rest of the day: 'ka tle here di' [May the rest of the day be good]. It is generally rare to hear a situation where someone who is greeted responds by providing negative or unpleasant news, answer or information. The answer to a greeting is always positive, in Jula and in many other African cultures. That leads to comments like the following: "an African will always say s/he is well, although they are unwell". This is not an oddity since the real news can be given or shared after the greeting. Hence the following conclusion by Wojtowicz: "One is not expected to give a negative answer or to elaborate on the real condition. In other words, a greeting should not be regarded as an instance of free conversation, all it shows is an attitude of the speaker, as it is used to express one's feelings toward the hearer." Another feature that illustrates the importance of greetings in Jula is the synonymity between 'greeting' and 'visiting'. The same word, 'fo' can be used for either of them, so greeting is as important as paying someone a visit. It is necessary to point out that certain differences exist among African languages, in realm of greetings. In certain African cultures, a greeting can be an opportunity to mention or explain one's problems. Speakers of Yoruba, Ewe and Hausa contend that it is acceptable to talk about one's troubles as an answer to a general greeting. Among the Hausa especially, if one of the participants (in the greeting process) feels like complaining, the hearer will not be surprised, and will listen and sympathize with those who have problems. In those 3 cultures and languages, greetings can be the occasion to communicate ideas, unlike Jula where greetings play a role of phatic communication.

In the case of South Africa in general, it is important to greet everyone respectfully and immediately upon seeing them. This is especially important in rural areas, where it is respectful to greet everyone you pass by. The most common greeting is a handshake accompanied with eye contact and a smile. Some overlook the importance of greeting now, most of the time they explain their attitude with the importance of 'modernity' or the mimicry of western ways. That might account for the fracas that occurred between South African rapper Nasty C and Ghanaian rapper Sarkodie. The media reveals that the refusal to shake hands caused that serious acrimony: "South African rapper Nasty C has revealed that he has refused to feature on a song with Ghanaian rapper Sarkodie for personal reasons. Nasty C said he turned down two feature offers from Sarkodie because he resented the way the Ghanaian rapper treated him when they first met. Nasty C revealed that the 'Non-Living Things' artist refused to shake his hand and he vowed never to give him a verse". This shows how the significance of greeting affects all aspects of life, from an ordinary encounter on a road or street to the show biz set, relationships or collaborations.

HIP HOP, NATIONAL AND PANAFRICAN IDENTITY IN BURKINA FASO

The Dawn of the Movement

As I alluded to in the previous entry on Music and Dance in Burkina Faso, hip hop and rap music found their way into that country around the 1980s and took a special twist when artists from different angles, backgrounds, and skills created a special *métissage* that combined hip hop, choreography, and acting in movies. This piece focuses on the correlation between the revolutionary Africanist wind that blew over the country of the incorruptible person during the 1983-1987 revolution spearheaded by Thomas Sankara. I also look at the social dimension of this artistic movement and related crucial values like Africanity, the African personality, and others.

Influence of Sankara's revolution and the black diaspora

The concept and praxis of Blackness at its core of hip hop facilitated the propagation of this genre in certain spheres in the world, especially the African continent. The central place of hip hop in Burkina and in Ouagadougou precisely cannot be underrated, and one of the proofs of that sovereignty is the International Waga Hip-Hop Festival that has been in existence since the year 2000. Hip hop was initially anchored in the notions of the subaltern and identity, and also transnational commonalities. It is interesting to contemplate what the concepts of Blackness and National Culture represent today in Burkina. Rap and hip-hop stress black consciousness and the knowledge of, and pride in, black history within many artistic circles in Ouagadougou. Rap has therefore been Africanized through the texts/messages it is based on, as well as the musical instruments it uses. Rap gained momentum in Burkina in the 1990s, when the youth that was fond of it started wearing baggy jean trousers, basket shoes, caps turned the other way, large tee-shirts, and also special habits like ways of greeting one another, as well as ways of speaking. The striking coincidence in all this is the regain of national and black pride in Burkina and Thomas Sankara's revolution that echoed many of those same values: the creation of a new culture, with the construction of national unity in mind, within a context where the following strong symbols exist: a new national anthem, new colors for the national flag, and a re-baptism of the country that drops the colonial or neocolonial name Upper Volta; the role of the artist therefore became to steadfastly convey national ideals. This falls into a larger picture and opinion where the artist, whilst being informed by the nation, is indeed above the nation. That also means that the artist is able to take the nation and people to task, see into the future what the nation and people are not aware of, and push new ways of seeing and thinking to the nation. Sankara became an icon during and after his life; in the year 2000 and beyond, numerous rap artists mention him in their songs. The history of rap in Burkina, therefore, unveils the existence of close links between the effort to assert a national culture soaked in a pan Africanist spirit on one hand, and on the other hand, an appropriation of the codes and ways of Black America as it was done by some hip-hop fans in Ouagadougou. The observer can notice that in some of the activities of The French Cultural Center in Ouagadougou (Centre Cultural Français), which used to organize contests and shows in which the famous rap artist Smokey (Serge Bambara) could already be seen as a star to be. One thing that galvanized the fans of rap at that time was race: African

Americans and French Africans (mulattos) were considered to be Africans, and the Burkinabè preferred listening to the songs of the French Africans and Caribbean artists. To the Burkinabè, Black diasporans had succeeded in imposing themselves on the artistic and both socio-political and socio-cultural scene of the West. For Burkinabè rap artists, to hold the microphone and perform on stage was a sign of success and power; it meant that although they had not traveled to the Americas or Europe, they could sing as well as their diasporan counterparts.

Some Catalysts

When investigative journalist Norbert Zongo was assassinated in 1998 while he was writing on crimes, embezzlements, and atrocities of the Compaoré regime, the latter became less popular and made some concessions. Some degree of freedom of speech was set in, and the first studio for recording hip-hop music was set up by Smokey. A new Art World was born and coexisted with rap. In that newly founded circle, one still finds rap singers, producers, managers, artists, journalists, and sponsors.

Movies and cinematography contributed to the "molding" of several Burkinabè rap artists. Smarty is one of such persons, and he clearly states that watching charismatic and influential black personalities like Malcolm X, Ray Charles, and excellent African leaders like Lumumba ignited his love for rap. He concludes by saying that the same love of rap led him to do more research on culture and politics, a habit that helped him acquire some knowledge that does not always exist within the confines of a classroom. Malkom, a member of the rap band Faso Kombat, picked that name up because of his love for Malcolm X.

Rap has always been in Africa and it originated in Africa. This musical genre expressed in Burkina the realities of the life of Blacks throughout the world, the history of their struggles, and the knowledge of Pan-Africanism, if we understand pan Africanism to be the relation between continental Africa and its diaspora.

STRIKE FEVER IN GHANAIAN UNIVERSITIES

For almost a month in 2024, workers' strike was the main thing in the sector of higher education in Ghana. That can easily be explained, when one remembers that workers' unions and workers' demands generate a halt of work, when these two clash. Certain unions and certain nations or countries have a reputation as "hard nut to crack" while others are known for their weak or almost null resistance or resilience. The British used to be known as a nation where labor unions are efficient when it comes to defending the interests of their members. That could probably be traced to the early solid culture of industrialization that comes with a number of factory workers and employees of a similar category. In France also, the various trade unions have a reputation for asserting their dissatisfaction. The recent avalanche of demonstrations that the yellow vests unleashed on the streets of France and the fury of the farmers against the reforms around the agriculture sector are a case in point, still in France. A general brief review of the situation shows that countries with a higher practice of liberalism and private enterprise are the ones with limited unions in general. When the practice is that one can be hired and fired as the employer wills, the desire to down tools reduces.

In the case of Ghana, the prevailing economic situation which is a cause of concern for many could but generate such a "shake up". The economy of the country is in one of the worst states that have ever been experienced, apart from the years of the gaping unnerving corruption that preceded the 1979 coup d'etat which is said to have brought some degree of sanity in the system. Historians and political scientists are still writing on that topic and views are different when it comes to that coup and its anti-corruption edge. What cannot be denied is that the overage citizen in Ghana is finding it almost impossible to make ends meet and vices, immorality and debauchery that follow such dire straits have emerged, and keep growing. Several words are used, in the attempt to refer to the debacle of the current Ghanaian socio-economic and political situation: a power of revenge, the rule of an ethnic group, the leadership style of the national bourgeois and much more.

I am of the view that strong and vibrant unions are necessary and should leap into action when the conditions of the union members require a manifestation of discontent. The repression of trade unions and the inaction of unions is one of the worst situations for workers. Management of the main universities of the country (University of Ghana (UG), University of Media, Arts and Communications (UniMAC), and University for Development Studies (UDS), among others, therefore had to issue statements announcing the postponement of their reopening dates. Classes were to resume between late September and mid-October 2024 according to the various calendars of the institutions, but the strike action led to an indefinite postponement of school reopening. In general, the key units or functions of the universities have been affected, besides the postponement of reopening date: Delays in salary payments, interruptions to IT services, postponement of graduation schedules, admissions into the universities being disrupted and High School graduates having to wait longer. A disturbance in the university reopening has numerous other repercussions since important changes will have to be done on the academic calendar when work resumes. Parents certainly become anxious since the preparations (psychological and financial) planned or invested for their wards' academic year or semester will have to be reconsidered; citizens living on businesses related to students' presence on campus (stationary shops operators, food vendors, etc.) are frustrated, idle with an interrupted source of income. Tertiary education in general and university hospitals' services will be disrupted and demonstrations near public universities and government building should not be excluded. Then, should students join the movement with time (since the strike affects them directly), the scale of the demonstrations and associated risk of clashes with security forces will likely increase. Some observers opine that the timing of the strike is well-chosen since reopening, which is one of the most important events on every school or university calendar is being affected. Postponing school reopening has a plethora of ripple effects and to top it all, 2024 is an election year in the country. The government's reaction has important repercussions.

The unions behind the industrial action are known in general as those of universities administrators: the Senior Staff Association of Universities of Ghana, Ghana Association of University Administrators (GAUA), Teachers and Educational Workers Union (TEWU). The media puts the current situation in these words "industrial actions turn universities into "ghost towns"". The demands behind the strike are the dissatisfaction of the workers of the unions mentioned above: the government's failure to pay negotiated and approved allowances because while new rates for allowances have been agreed upon by the various parties, many university administrators are still paid old rates, while others receive no payment. Vehicle maintenance and pensions allowances are frequently mentioned in the discussion.

Other tentacles are emerging from the university administrators' strike: Organized Labor, which is the umbrella organization of all the unions planned a nation-wide strike on Thursday 10th October 2024 but ultimately called it off on October 9, "after having assessed the situation on the terrain" as they said. In other words, there was improvement and hope in the attitude of the government. The main reason for Organized Labor to join the strike was the unacceptable and suicidal state that illegal mining commonly called "galamsey" has reached in the country. Sources from Ghana Water Company allegedly stated that 30% or less of the water to be supplied to the population is fit for consumption since more than 70% contains heavy metals like mercury, arsenic, and lead, a perfect recipe for toxicity or water poisoning. The water bodies of Ghana have almost all been destroyed, and that planned strike action was aiming at addressing the flail. Calling it off took many people by surprise and time will hopefully reveal more on the reasons. But the issue of illegal mining is still stirring much controversy. On Thursday October 10, the University Teachers Association of Ghana (UTAG) had declared an unlimited nation-wide strike due to the damages of illegal mining. Speculations lead to some degree of reservation about this nation-wide strike of the University Teachers Association. The body explains its action with the fact that Organized Labor disappointed by rescinding their call to strike, since, to UTAG, no tangible reason could explain such volte face.

What started as a dissatisfaction of the university administrators is taking an apparently complex dimension, that could imply hidden agendas (let us remain mindful of the fact that presidential elections are by the corner and as usual, national and individual ambitions manifest themselves in many forms). What makes many ponder more is the following recurring question: Why such a special concern over illegal mining at this specific moment when the phenomenon has been with Ghanaians for years? Is illegal mining being fought in the appropriate manner since it is no secret that high official governments are behind it? UTAG could certainly say that as a body of academics, no one could be more concerned or vocal on something that has now turned into a "national tragedy". Others believe that different reasons explain this nation-wide strike declared by UTAG and they add that illegal mining is just a façade. Parochial interests are the genuine reason, according to many citizens. These dimensions of the strike(s) have to be closely monitored since surprises or novel elements or dimensions always pop up.

THE TRUTH BEHIND SCHOOL TEXTBOOKS IN FRENCH SPEAKING AFRICA: WESTERN-DRIVEN CONTENT AND MARKET

French speaking Africa is still running an education system that is bedeviled by a horrendous combination of two misfortunes: a totally colonized content of textbooks and the production of those textbooks is the preserve of Western countries, precisely two institutions: The World Bank and the International Monetary Fund (IMF). The reflection and analysis in this piece is based on reliable sources.

Kenyan Novelist Ngugi wa Thiong'o generally come to our mind when we ponder the education system of formerly colonized countries and the mental state of the students to whom those books are taught. He put his concern in 2 statements which are the following: "The white man (colonizer) is gone but he left behind a textbook that functions as a perfect surrogate white master". He later theorized the machinery that distorts the thinking and decision-making ability of the so-called independent people in a seminal book titled *Decolonizing the Mind* (1986). A simple look at the textbook production and the budget behind it unfortunately corroborate Ngugi's concerns. Research unveils that 90% of school textbooks in French-speaking Africa or Francophone Africa comes from France. These materials are written by French citizens who were sent to Africa or chose to reside in Africa for a while (months or years) and write reading materials or Arithmetic textbooks and more. Those books are written in France, by French people and they are produced by French publishing houses.

The most common textbook for the teaching of Reading in Basic School in Francophone Africa used to be *Mamadou et Bineta*, which is still used in certain countries although it was replaced by other similar books in certain countries. Names of persons in those books are African names, generally like Kojo, Kokou, Fanta, Amina, Koffi, etc. and activities are similar to the following: Pierre et Karim vont au marigot (Pierre/Peter and Kareem are going to the river), Delphine joue avec ses amies (Delphina is playing with her friends), La rentrée des classes (School reopening day), Les chaussures du roi Makoko (King Makoko's shoes) and much more; these are the closest English translations of the French titles. These are texts that are written by Westerners, so African students who study such manuals in school learn to look at or to view/see the world, through the lens of a French man or French culture; only the names are African. Therefore, the students thoroughly engage or imbibe a Westerner's reading (French in his case) of the African culture. This means that the mind of Africans is conditioned or programmed in a manner chosen by a white French person or the psyche and mind / brain of the African is molded or programmed in a such a way that it functions the way the French citizen wants it to function. The textbook therefore becomes an agent of destruction, of control or defeat which is more powerful and more wicked than the European colonizer. Another important detail is that the school manuals in French-speaking Africa are produced by two (exactly and solely) publishing companies which are: *Hachette Livre* or *Hachette* in general (founded in Paris in 1826) and Hatier, founded in 1880, with headquarters in Paris.

The business behind this mental conditioning or utter objectification process is clearly captured in this study by UNESCO which concludes that 15% of the budget of the education sector in French-speaking African countries is allocated to textbooks and all those books are made in France. Many critics who, most of time, claim that "Africans are lazy, since they cannot produce textbooks or school manuals for themselves" and such people generally go further and ask "what prevents Africans from stressing entrepreneurship and putting in place publishing houses that produce school manuals written by Africans and for Africans? Is France responsible for all the misfortunes of Africa? In this specific case, the answer is "yes". The truth is that the economic situation of Africa is said to compel African countries to subsidize school manuals. Textbooks are sold in local bookshops at a price which is half of the cost of the book when it is sold by the French publisher. So, governments purchase them at a high cost from France and sell them to students or parents at a much reduced and subsidized cost. A book that costs 5,000 CFA francs (8.5 USD) on the African marker was probably bought more than 10,000 CFA francs (17 USD) by the African state or government from the publisher. In such a case, the State is the main buyer or importer and the bookshops get their commodities from the State.

The funds for this subsidy come from "loans" that African countries obtain from the World Bank and the IMF as I intimated initially. Now the other trick is that those moneys are not directly sent to the accounts or coffers of the African states. The IMF and World Bank transfer the funds directly into the coffers of the French publishing companies that in turn send the books to the African countries. So, for 60 years (since the "end" of colonization), Africans have been paying for the subsidization of school textbooks, produced by French companies and sold at a high cost, with no competitor, since they are the only ones allowed and chosen to produce the books.

African countries therefore cannot choose to purchase the manuals from a different book publisher of their choice (it could be a European, Australian Canadian publisher, etc.) whose prices are lower and whose books have the contents required by national curricula of African countries. Many non-Africa countries follow that practice: As long as the content of a textbook matches the curriculum, the book is purchased from that publisher once the price is reasonable for their budget. In the US for instance, districts are free to purchase their school manuals from a publisher, as long as the content is the required one and the price is good for them. In the case of Africa, two financial giants dictate the text producer and that could explain the choice of the directors of those two institutions. The IMF is almost always led by a French citizen and the World bank has an American (US) director. So, the wealthy Western institutions trade among themselves, using Africa as an asset in that financial game.

The patriotic African educator and entrepreneur who sets up their publishing house (because they have discovered the exploitation of the French) will go bankrupt because their books will certainly be of a better content, highly Afromorphous but the production cost of the textbooks will certainly call for a market price which will be higher, simply because such books will not be subsidized by the state. As a result, parents or students will patronize books made in France because they are more affordable, since the African government bears part of the costs. The African state will simply tell the African publisher that the state does not have the money to subsidize his (African publisher) books, since the money for the subsidization of the books comes from the IMF and World Bank and ends up in the hands of the French publisher, leaving Africans with only huge debts to pay. So, the consumption or purchasing habit of Africans is controlled by the debt (loan system), an apparatus that enriches Western institutions, a plain display of the innermost system of neocolonialism. For 60 years, Hachette and Hatier publishing houses have been cashing in billions, without any special effort. The only explanation that could be given is that their country, France colonized ours, in Africa. UNESCO published that "the exportation of textbooks to French-speaking African countries enabled the two French publishers to cash in five hundred billion CFA francs (500 billion CFA francs or about 847,007,284 USD) during ten years, and that means 50 billion CFA francs or roughly 84,690,325 USD) each year.

Several loopholes have been detected and debated, around the quality of education in Africa in general, and the neocolonial influence on the education system, and that second factor is said to more pronounced in French-speaking Africa. Not so much was apparently known about the pro-France economic policy. It would be worthy finding out if a similar unjust intellectual and mercantile policy exists in English speaking Africa.

DEADLY ALCOHOLIC DRINKS IN BURKINA FASO: MORGUES THAT ARE PATRONIZED

Alcohol consumption has always been one of the social ills that several institutions have tried to combat. According to the World Health Organization (WHO), alcohol consumption killed 3, 3 million people in 2012, and illegally produced alcohol or *alcool frélaté* in French represents 25% of the alcohol drunk in the world in 2016. Burkina Faso is no exception; the phenomenon is taking a more twisted and alarming dimension, which combines sadness and humor, a tragicomedy that pounced on the nation and is aggressively decimating it.

New Meaning for "Morgue"

The term is used to refer to spots where adulterated alcohol, *alcool frélaté*, a deadly drink which is forbidden by the law, is sold. It comes in many types, and these are some of the names it bears: Château de France, Jack et Daniel, Beaufort, tchirou-tchirou, raccourcis, sap-sap, pissance, cerceuil, mal guaré, etc. The first three are names of highly regarded wines and beers in the French/ Francophone society; the last three mean, respectively, in accurate French translation: shortcut, fast, power, coffin, and wrong parking. These drinks are, to the naked eye, in little quantities packaged in sachets and sealed. The little quantity does not mean that its effect is weak; the alcohol content in them is extremely high. Customers testify that they get real satisfaction from these drinks that are sold everywhere in Burkina, from the cities to rural areas. The kiosks where they are sold are called 'morgues', a coherent synonymous with the hospital morgue, since those who patronize these drinks are ultimately victims of terminal diseases like liver failure, heart attack. All in all, more than 200 types of diseases that affect the human brain, the cardiovascular system, cancer, damage of the GI tract (intestine), maladies, etc., are effects of the consumption of adulterated alcohol. Some of the customers are young men who graduated from professional schools and universities and cannot find a job. As a result, these drinks end up causing tensions between young men and their parents, and also between couples. A study revealed an impressive solidarity among those who go to the morgue, since one can get the adulterated stuff on credit, and the price is very low. The expensive whisky and wine were once imported from foreign countries, but now, the adulterated ones are locally produced by people who have no reliable knowledge of the production of alcoholic beverages, and there is no guarantee that they master the various ingredients that go into the genuine ones. The deadly, illegal, and adulterated alcohol started as an imported product, coming from Ghana and Cameroon around 1990, before the local production started. Those who sell these drinks are said to cash in on a 100% profit. This social malaise seems to have reached its peak today in Burkina.

These addicted ones are so familiar with the drinks that with closed eyes or just by taking a sip, they can tell the exact brand or name of the drink. We are mentioning young men most of the time here because girls and women who consume illegal substances in Burkina most of the time are rich women, sometimes of loose morals, or prostitutes who sniff cocaine. Women seem to be a real minority in the consumption of adulterated alcohol. Burkinabe social media cites a research that poses that in the same situation, only one woman said that she drinks "grenade", a drink that makes her feel like a superhuman being.

Who are the Clients?

A team of journalists infiltrated a kiosk and described their experience in these words: Whisky, pastis, mangoustan, alomo, gin, all in sachets, and many others are what the owner serves to his customers. The regular customers know one another, and we had to convince them that we are not outsiders by ordering two shots of whisky as soon as we entered the kiosk. We looked around and decided to sit close to a man who was alone, on a bench. He was more than 40 years old, with sinking eyeballs and red lips. He looked at us with suspicion and did not greet us in return when we greeted him. In order to break this hostility, we bought him some pastis, since his glass was almost empty. That did the trick. The man told us 'Thank you very much, my brothers, God bless you. Then, during our conversation, we got to know that he was a family man with a troubled life. His wife left him one day, going away with their children, and in search of solace, our interlocutor took to drinking adulterated alcohol. To him, the reasons behind this addiction are: joblessness, poverty, sorrows, stress, the search for pleasure, and also bad company. Another tableau of woes unveils the sinister result of this addiction. A young man stated that in 10 years, he lost 8 friends to the deadly substance. Another one leads the journalists to the grave of one of his friends who fell, a victim of the thing. A citizen who was very vocal and against this 'killer' introduced his former classmate, and the latter is simply a bag of bones, standing on crutches, visibly someone who cannot use his legs anymore, wearing very dirty clothes, soaked in sweat. The classmate gave some coins to his former mate, who is now a beggar, living solely on and for the drink. The substance is known to kill more than malaria and HIV/AIDS in Burkina. Sopal, the national factory that produced alcohol from sugar cane, was closed down for being involved in the production of adulterated alcohol, and there is no doubt that Indians and Lebanese are the biggest producers of *alcool frélaté* in Burkina. India is known to be the epicenter of its production in the world. Burkina Faso is therefore far from the end of this tragedy that is eating into the core of her youth. Are the political authorities pulling their weight in this battle against the flail? That is what my next entry will address.

THE BUSINESS OF PHARMACEUTICAL FIRMS

Pharmaceutical firms and health research centers have been indicted severally. Many citizens deplore the lies, subjugation and business-oriented character of those institutions. Pandemics are fertile moments for that trait to surface or resurface. We very often hear that parasites, viruses or microbes have been "created" or "made" in laboratories and spread in such a way that they successfully afflict a targeted population. Generally, such a phenomenon reminds readers of the Frankenstein Monster, when something being worked on in a lab escapes the scientist's control and sets off to harm human beings. The most recent case is that of COVID-19, which generated many views, judgments, and speculations. The most common of those comments was that the virus behind that pandemic emerged from a laboratory in China; the speculation becomes more complex when we hear that the virus that escaped was the result of genuine research aiming to treat a certain ailment. Other sources condemn Chinese scientific institutions and other Western ones for having connived in the production of a virus that would kill a large number of people. That second speculation is difficult to believe since figures show that COVID killed more people in China and Western countries than it did in other parts of the world, especially Africa.

A medical tragedy which has been verified in world history is the Tuskegee Experiment, an unethical and racist clinical research conducted between 1932 and 1972 in Macon County, Alabama, in the US. There was then no known cure for syphilis, a contagious venereal disease and 600 African American men were used as guinea pigs in a scientific project that aimed to study the progression of the disease.

The African American men were deceived by a team of medical doctors who told them that they were being offered free health care against 'bad blood, ' a term used to refer to many ailments at that time. The 600 men (399 of them had latent syphilis and the control group was 201 persons) who are now known to have been victims were obviously from a poor background and many of them had never visited a medical doctor before. The physicians involved achieved their sadistic aim since the men's fate was: death, blindness, insanity and many other complications related to untreated syphilis. The cruelty against those men led 15 years later, in 1947 to penicillin being the recommended prescription for the treatment of syphilis. That incident might be the reason why many blacks in the Americas and Africa were reluctant to receive the COVID-19 vaccine. Many cases of such medical injustice can be found in world history.

Dengue fever (or break-bone fever) which was first recorded in Africa in 1779 and the West Indies in 1635, resurfaced this year and is claiming lives. The areas affected by the endemic are the Americas, Africa, Asia, the Middle East and the Pacific Islands. In Burkina Faso for instance, the September 2023 statistics reveal that approximately 3,335 cases were recorded and 31 people died. Burkina is one of the countries known for frequent outbreaks of the fever while countries like Chad, Cameroon and many others are known for sporadic or uncertain outbreaks and 20,000 deaths are recorded every year worldwide. That viral infection is transmitted by the bites of infected mosquitoes (Aedes mosquitoes that also transmit the Zika virus). Unfortunately, there is no known and certain cure for dengue fever, and the following are recommended to alleviate the pain and increase chances of recovery: having enough rest, drinking a lot of fluid, taking paracetamol, and avoiding non-steroidal anti-inflammatory drugs like ibuprofen. Juice, concoctions, and infusions from fresh pawpaw leaves, lime and honey, kiwifruit, pomegranate, and apple are recommended. Dengue fever cannot be cured; only the symptoms can be treated. Kiwifruit is highly recommended because it contains abundant vitamins E, C, K, and zinc.

Dengue fever like malaria, is caused by a certain type of mosquito, and each of these two diseases kills people: while 99% of people who contract dengue fever ultimately recover, millions of malaria patients die, especially children in Africa. The general information is that there is no completely effective vaccine for malaria, only treatments that cure patients are available. The aggressive upsurge of dengue fever in Burkina led to talks about a vaccine invented some years ago by a Burkinabè medical researcher, Professor Halidou TINTO. His research activities are known to have focused on malaria parasite biology and the epidemiology of resistance and clinical trials for new drugs and vaccines. That researcher, who trained in Belgium, has the background of a pharmacist and worked in several research institutes (Africa and Europe) and won "The Name in Science 2021 Award" in Oxford, UK. Professor TINTO's malaria vaccine was to be administered to children, from 5 years and below, since children are the majority of the people killed by malaria. Unfortunately, the vaccine was not accredited or homologated by the World Health Organization (WHO), so it could not be used. The same sources contend that now that dengue fever is ravaging a large number of people in humid areas and large cities in Burkina (it is a tropical disease), a strange coincidence is noticed: this is exactly the period when Professor TINTO's malaria vaccine is about to be accredited. Most people, therefore, believe that pharmaceutical companies will make a lot of profit. From now onwards, pharmaceutical companies in the West will work around the clock to produce a treatment against dengue fever, a product that will be sold in pharmacy shops. In other words, now that another threat is reigning, dengue fever, the previous one, which is malaria, can be eradicated by Professor TINTO's invention, and the energy, attention, and money of citizens in countries affected by dengue fever will be directed towards dengue fever medication. Many sales will be done because the shelves in pharmacies will be filled with that medicine, which people will have to purchase. So those pharmaceutical companies, firms, and industries are said to cash in on diseases and calamities that they strategically work to maintain, with the support and backing of the World Health Organization. Many discontent people refer to the WHO as a criminal organization. It is disheartening to realize that October 5, 2023, is the date when discussions started towards the validation of that malaria vaccine, and it might take, allegedly, 6 months to one year before it is approved, and the world will be able to talk about the eradication of malaria. That is no solace because a killer disease will replace another one. Dengue fever will settle in while malaria is gradually being effaced. Hence, pharmaceutical labs and firms will keep functioning and making a profit, while human lives are taken away. A specialist in solar energy who discloses his identity is very vocal about this analysis; although this may sound too speculative, the artist says in his own words that he strongly believes

258 | P a g e

that this deadly mercantile activity is led by those who do want the current Burkinabè "revolution" to succeed, since only a healthy people can unleash and sustain a revolution.

THE PROPHECY OF THE CHE GUEVARA OF AFRICA COMES TO PASS

It is not a secret that both Thomas Sankara of Burkina Faso and Che Guevara of Cuba (a native of Argentina) said several times that they could be assassinated, but their ideas would remain, so they predicted their immortality. Sankara said, "If you kill Sankara today, in the coming days you will have millions of Sankara". Guevara is known to have uttered that "if I am killed, they would have killed just a human being, but my ideas and ideals will remain and continue to affect the world youth and world politics". No wonder Sankara was referred to as the Che Guevara of Africa. In Cuba, Che Guevara's prediction came to pass when his ideas remained implanted on the island after his death, till today. During his funeral, his comrade-in-arms, Fidel Castro, said, "Our dearest wish for our children or younger generations is that they emulate Che. This South American freedom fighter became a world icon after he was gunned down by the US imperialism, the CIA precisely, through the Green Berets, a unit whose mission was to defeat guerilla warfare whose main "face" was Che, after Castro stayed in power in Havana and Che embarked on his propagation of the revolution in the world (Africa, other countries in South America like Bolivia where he met his demise, heroically). Che is a little bit like Bob Marley of Jamaica: the more their native land celebrates and tries to appropriate them, the more they escape their country and become global and world figures. Today, no space or object escapes that celebration fury of Che: from well-researched academic documents to streets, T-shirts, and cigarette lighters, Che's name and effigy are present.

In the same vein, the current political scene in Burkina is the exact confirmation of Thomas Sankara's visionary statement. The September 30th coup brought to power a Captain who strikingly has a lot of similarities with Thomas Sankara, and, the new junta leader captain Traoré (appointed as president since October 2022) and his first prime minister, Lawyer Joachim Kyelem de Tambela. The latter openly stated that the only path to get Burkina Faso out of the quagmire of economic chaos and terrorist insecurity is Sankara's ideas and vision.

It might help to point out that Sankara's anti-France sentiments have never been hidden. The Burkinabè TV program *Intégrité 226* featured, some months ago, a conversation between Rasmané Kientega, a young leader of the main Burkinabè trade Union, the General Confederation of Burkinabè Workers (CGT-B), and the French ambassador to Burkina, Luc Hallade, in 2019. The young, eloquent, brave, and intelligent interlocutor simply revealed to the ambassador how unhelpful his country has been to Burkina Faso. That debate is amazing for several reasons: the French ambassador started by saying that "the Burkina Faso army is in a phase of reconstruction and as such, it takes about 10 years for such an army to regain stability". The diplomat was certainly referring to the jihadist attacks that have been more than a nightmare for Burkina and other countries in the subregion. As Thomas Sankara would have done, the young trade unionist simply "shut" the French ambassador down with these words: "You are saying that our army is going through a reconstruction, and our army became a national army since 1960, when we became "independence". If such an old army, whose senior officers trained in France -more than the majority- and who is always "supported by military instructors from France is still in a period of reconstruction, that could mean 2 things: either you, France and her army is a bad instructor and teacher, or the student, the Burkinabè military trainees are bad students; but the answer is simple, since no government in Burkina has ever said that the national army is incompetent and in reconstruction". What the young man meant is that the ambassador spoke like a colonial master who does not speak carefully and throws the blame at the colonized. Mr. Hallade certainly thought that he was on a TV set with colonized Upper Volta people. His argument was destroyed, and he remained speechless throughout the whole program. This *Intégrité 226* Program, the attack against French public institutions just after the September 30th coup, confirms that Sankarism is back in Burkina Faso. The TV program and its background were breathtaking: while the young trade unionist "silenced" the French ambassador, a portrait picture of Sankara, in a calm, pensive, emotional, happy and but unsurprised mood hung in the upper right corner, like an angel up, looking at terrestrial events. Sankara seemed to be saying, "Yes, the time has come, my young disciples have started work, with the intellectual skills and lessons I left them with".

It might help to recall that between 1983 and 1987, France lost its grip over Burkina Faso. It all started with the change of name, from the neocolonial French name Haute Volta (Upper Volta) to the endogenous name Burkina Faso, a combination of two terms from two of the main languages spoken in the country (Mossi and Dioula / Jula), and which means the country of the incorruptible (or upright) person. The current regime in power claims to be that of the youth, much like the youngsters of the 1960s and 70s Upper Volta, who had thorough knowledge of political issues, and had a sizeable political consciousness. The TV program I referred to earlier was really one-sided and taught the French ambassador a lesson, which is the kind of act Sankara used to pose, almost daily. For instance, when former French president François Mitterrand visited Burkina Faso in November 1986, he was stunned by a couple of things: Burkina Faso was no longer part of "France's backyard", and Sankara was not the type of leader who bows to France. The man and his country had changed. Alexandra Reza in *Short Cuts* (December 2014) captures that new dynamics between Burkina and France in the following scene: "At the dinner with Mitterrand, Thomas Sankara is dressed in a royal blue captain's jacket with gold braid at the cuffs and the neck. He speaks without notes, his hands clasped behind his back. Mitterrand, by contrast, is drab and impassive in an ashen suit and tie. He looks straight ahead. Sankara berates the brazen insouciance of the French, who have no qualms about receiving visits from white supremacists and their allies: 'And so it is in this context, Monsieur François Mitterrand, that we have not understood how bandits such as Jonas Savimbi (the then Commander of Mozambican rebellion), killers like Pieter Botha (president of South Africa during Apartheid) have had the right to rove across France. They have stained it with their hands and with their feet, which are covered in blood. And all those who have allowed them to act as they have will carry the full responsibility, here and elsewhere, today and forever. The film cuts to Mitterrand, who has risen to respond. If he may be permitted to speak from the heights of his experience, he says, Sankara talks with the fine bravery of youth, but his tongue is too sharp and he goes too far. François places an avuncular hand on Thomas's shoulder. Sankara laughs but doesn't look up".

Less than a year later, in October 1987, Thomas Sankara was shot dead in his office along with 12 of his aides during a coup led by his former friend Blaise Compaoré and backed by France. But daily happenings in today's Burkina, obviously, point to one thing: Thomas Sankara's prediction of his "immortality" is a fact.

THE BEACON OF DEMOCRACY IN AFRICA IS DISAPPOINTING MANY

Senegal is known to be the Francophone West African country where democracy is part of the tradition. It is the beacon of democracy, as political analysts generally say. That can be understood since a coup d'état has never taken place in that country. The army knows that its place is in the barracks. Another fact that distinguishes Senegal is that it is really the backyard of France. Those ties started during the colonial era, when the French used that country as a 'watch tower'. Military operations that aimed at rounding up and training African troops for the Second World War, the Indochina war, and the French war in Algeria relied on Senegalese politicians (Blaise Diagne is one of them), and the Senegalese soil was used to marshal soldiers for the war. During World War Two, the West African soldiers who came to the rescue of France against Nazi Germany were brought to Senegal from all the French colonies. They fought so well on the war front and were called Senegalese riflemen, although not all of them were from Senegal.

Strategically, France built its training institutions in Senegal. Dakar, Saint Louis, and many other cities were the location of important institutions like the William Ponty teachers' college for West Africa, the military academy, and the premier university, Cheikh Anta Diop University. Many African intellectuals and officers are products of these tertiary institutions. The Ivorian first president, Houphouet Boigny, and famous Ivorian writer Bernard Dadié, trained in that college, as well as the first presidents of Mali, Niger, Upper Volta, etc. Cheikh Anta Diop University was the best institution where those who aspired to university education could find themselves. That prestige is still alive. Despite the general crisis of education in Africa, those who train at that university are highly regarded.

Since France had so many vital institutions in that country, it had to control its political life. The first president of Senegal, the academic Leopold Sedar Senghor trained in Paris and ended up teaching French in France, and also worked for the academy of the French language, the gatekeeper for the sanctity of the language. No wonder, unlike English, words cannot be coined and introduced into French easily. While we have world English or Global English, there is only one 'type' or variety of French, officially: that which respects the rules laid down by the French Language Academy. Senegalese political personalities were accepted as parliamentarians in French. That rapport between France and Senegal created a frame of mind in the average contemporary Senegalese citizen. The influence of France is resilient, and in general, Senegalese citizens see themselves as French citizens, except that Wolof (the predominant language in the country) is their favorite medium of communication. Eating habits and many other basic practices in Senegal are totally tailored following the French model. Needless to say that the largest businesses are owned by French nationals.

With such a socio-political atmosphere prevailing, the Western model of democracy easily found its way into the country, and the army never meddled in politics. But that democratic image is currently going through some changes, and many are wondering where the roots of such a change emanate from, in a country where peaceful transition is the norm: Senghor, the first president handed over to his prime minister Abdou Diouf who in turn handed over to Abdoulaye Wade through elections and then the reigns of governance landed in the hands of the immediate past president Macky Sall after some elections. During all those decades, only a few skirmishes took place. One instance is when Abdoulaye Wade wanted to maneuver for the election of his son, Karim Wade, whom the Senegalese did not want as president, partly because of his remoteness from the local political realities. He was seen as a bourgeois young man born to a Senegalese father and a white French mother. Surprisingly, for the first time, people have taken to the streets, and clashes between them and law enforcement forces have become too frequent and worrisome. And the person who generates such historical malaise is Ousmane Sonko, a 49-year-old former tax inspector who is the face of the opposition. His portrait can be summed up in these lines: a young politician, former mayor of one of the main cities (Ziguinchor), and opposed to the heavy control of France over the country. He is often seen to be more radical, sides with the poor and downtrodden, and is liked a lot by the youth, whose aspirations he shares and defends. He lost to the current president during the last elections in 2019 and is gearing up for the next ones, those of 2024, and his political party is Patriots of Senegal for Ethics, Work and Fraternity (PASTEF), founded in 2014. In 2016, he was perceived as a tax inspector-turned-whistleblower, since he exposed the illegal practices of the Senegalese elite and several international companies that used shady practices to avoid paying an estimated USD 8.9 million in taxes. Sonko was then terminated as a result of his activism.

There is allegedly a robust, tireless, and canning opposition to Sonko's election. France is said to be the main force behind that treatment Sonko and his partisans are facing. Senegal has a considerable oil reserve whose exploitation is to start in 2024, so the winner of the coming elections will handle the consumption and sale of that lucrative resource. The incumbent, Macky Sall, was pro-France and is said to be working towards the election of someone who shares his political stance, which is the unconditional defense of French interests in Senegal. Others go to the extent of stating that President Sall is trying to contest for a third term, something which is not allowed by the national constitution.

The campaign against Ousmane Sonko's participation in the 2024 elections took several forms, and some of them are openly "embarrassing" to some extent. He was accused and tried in April for raping a masseuse (Adji Sarr) in a massage salon, and was also said to have intimidated with death threats the 20-year-old masseuse. The rape charges were later dropped, and the opposition leader was sentenced to 2 years ' imprisonment, a fact that will "cripple" him politically, since he will not be able to contest for the coming elections. He was under house arrest for some time, and his partisans kept agitating vibrantly against those actions of the government in power. One of the main French media, *Radio France Internationale* (RFI), is said to have aired giant full anti-Sonko programs, but the onward march for the voice of the Senegalese opposition and the radical anti-imperialist who is also the voice of the voiceless was still on. Senegal has secured a peaceful and democratic reputation that it would gain in working to preserve. Falling into the camp of the

Pronunciamientos-familiar countries will be a big downward fall for that country.

CELEBRATION OF CRAFTSMANSHIP IN BURKINA FASO

SIAO is the main arts festival in Burkina Faso. It gives the opportunity to artisans from Africa, Asia, and Europe to showcase their handiwork, to trade and represent their countries, and also strike up friendships and business relationships. The acronym means *Salon International de l'Artisanat de Ouagadougou* or International Crafts Fair of Ouagadougou. It was born in 1984, from the will of the Burkinabè political authorities who realized that handicrafts contributed strongly to the growth of African economies in the same way as agriculture does. It began with an exhibition and sale of handicrafts in 1984, and was established as a full-fledged festival in 1990 with the participation of about thirty African countries. It is often referred to as *la vitrine de l'artisanat* or the showcase of craftmanship and enables also other vital and interrelated activities like auditing, consulting, and training in the field of craftmanship. A series of workshops is held on issues related to the production and promotion of artwork abroad, and instructors or presenters are selected from distinguished resource persons. The fair is organized every two (2 years, and to many, it is the ideal framework for African artisans who market their products on national and international markets. And the Burkinabè national authorities provided it with an administrative structure in order to improve the organization of the festival. This biennale of African handicrafts also encourages and facilitates the organization of artistic, cultural, and commercial events on the site. SIAO rewards creativity and a special pavilion called the Creativity Pavilion selects and exhibits the best products of each edition. The festivals also set up a jury composed of experts and professionals of international renown who select high-quality handcrafted products, marketable for export. Nothing is left out and the festival keeps improving from over the years and at its current stage, one of the impressive additions to SIAO is the "B to B wing" or pavilion, a framework for sharing experience and partnership, a real structure which is responsible for connecting professional buyers (wherever they come from) with local craftsmen in order to promote and grow craftsmanship. The festival's framework is a real architectural gem, which covers an area of approximately 7 hectares, made up of 3 air-conditioned pavilions, 2 ventilated pavilions, and 1 pavilion of creativity. The structure also comprises 2 bonded warehouses, 1 meeting room, 1 conference room, a restaurant area, and a children's play area. SIAO boasts of a Fashion Alley, which offers a mixture of materials, colors, effects, and original cuts, the climax of dazzling fashion. The best of African fashion and attire is exhibited there, through splendid stuff worn by the Tuareg, Fulani, Maasai, and Berber ethnic groups. The Flavors Gallery is patronized by fans of mouth-watering drinks. Original sumptuous, irresistible flavors attest to the presence of *tchapalo* (special brewed millet alcohol), *degué* (millet flour specially granulated and softly cooked, dipped into lightly sour milk with sugar, at low temperature), néré, shea juice, and kinkeliba juice. The last 3 products are mostly and generally known for their medicinal virtues, but this fair puts up their delicacy attributes. The Arts Gallery brings together bronzers, ceramists, potters, and stylists who master their skills. It gathers works of art that are not only original, unique, and rare but are also prized by collectors and discerning amateurs. SIAO succeeds in showing the beautiful, pleasant, useful, nutritious, and delicious products and materials of the terrain, precisely of Africa.

The following are some of the types of products that are exhibited during the festival, for the satisfaction of buyers or art fans from mere admirers to scholars in artistic creation; this list resonates with many of the craft objects lodged at the Arts Gallery: Sculpture (wood, bronze), leather goods, textile and clothing, "vannerie", embroidery, pottery (ceramics), armory, musical instruments, jewelry, decoration objects, ironwork, weaving, batik, recovery craftsmanship and furniture.

The 2022 edition was a special one since it occurred in a context of political transition, in a country that has been the victim of jihadist attacks for almost a decade. That context of insecurity caused this SIAO edition, which was initially scheduled between 28 October and 6 November 2022, to be postponed since the 2 coups d'état contributed to heightening the panic caused by the daily Al-Qaeda related terrorist attacks. Finally, the 16th edition of the International Crafts Fair of Ouagadougou (SIAO) was held from January 27 to February 6, 2023, under the theme: "African crafts, lever of development and factor of resilience of populations". The most crucial or central aspect of this edition was security, and fortunately, that was not deficient, and the current Director General of the festival, Mr. Dramane Tou, expressed the capability that Burkina showed, especially during the period of the SIAO. His statement combines a gratification to African ancestries (a perfect fit for such an event) and the general goals of all editions, and these were his words: "Thanks to the divine blessing, the ghosts of the ancestors and the blessings of all, we had the chance to organize a 16th edition in good condition. The report is positive because we were lucky enough to have quite interesting results in terms of the participation of the key players who are the craftsmen, in terms of the participation of the general public, and terms of the participation of the men and women of the press". For 10 days, craftsmen from all over the world were strongly mobilized, and figures confirm that 3,600 of them were present, plus 50 accredited media, 500 journalists, and 360,000 visitors trooped in every day. Besides the creativity side, the commercial dimension also favored both buyers who came from numerous countries and continents and the economy of the host country. 30 professional buyers were present, and the organizing committee was sure that they would break the record of 805 million CFA in revenue. SIAO aims to be the world's largest fair for African crafts. Participants came from 21 countries in Africa, Asia, Europe, and the Americas, with roughly 700 stands. One would not be overambitious by stating that this 16th edition of the SIAO is that of resilience, the resilience of an event that has stood the test of time since its establishment some thirty years ago, the resilience of a people who have always known how to stand up proudly to face the vagaries and other vicissitudes of life. This event, over the years, has established itself as one of the major attractions (almost characteristics now) of "the country of upright men" of which it is also one of the showcases, in the same way as the FESPACO (Pan-African Film and Television Festival of Ouagadougou), and the International Cycling Tour of Faso, to name but a few. The two festivals were occurring that year, just a few days apart. Ouagadougou is undeniably the mecca of black art, at least for some time.

SKIN BLEACHING: A PRACTICE LOSING GROUND IN AFRICA

Skin bleaching is not a new phenomenon, and it seems to have been used for centuries by humans. It takes many forms and relies on various means. While some people use certain pomades in order to lighten their skin, others use pills or injections, etc. If the means are diverse, one factor nonetheless remains the common denominator of all these means used to "bleach" one's skin: the longing for a lighter skin which itself stems from either an inferiority complex, a situation where an individual is ashamed of their skin color, or a desire to obtain some prestige like "fitting" within a certain social class or attracting the admiration of some people.

Skin bleaching exists on all the continents, among all races, and the majority of people who buy into this "metamorphosis" are blacks, browns (mulattoes and Latinos), and the yellow (term for Asians in general). The last two nouns were used for the first time by proponents of race theories around the 19th century, like the French Arthur de Gobineau and others. In the US, for instance, within the black community, skin bleaching is also called "passing", since it allows one person to pass for or as another person. In other words, a dark-skinned person who bleaches or whitens their skin often succeeds in doing it so well that society looks at that person as white. That practice is at the center of several cases that made history, since celebrated white persons were ultimately found to be blacks who passed as whites. In Asia, a light-skinned person has more prestige in general, and many people indulge in the practice. The attraction to the other one pops up here since we often realize that Caucasians in general are attracted to the dark-skinned or tanned ones. Speculations classify this as an offshoot of the "exotic", or the curiosity for the unknown. The sexual attraction between such people is explained by the concept of the exotic, a term that often relates to the denigration of the unknown and inferior race or skin color.

The attraction of a white male to a black female has been observed as a romantic phenomenon or as a mere curiosity of the whites towards the races they "conquered" or colonized, some notions that I reject as mere fallacies, an apologia to justify imperialism and pillage. In Literature, Joseph Conrad's *Heart of Darkness* (1899) presents a case or instance of such attractions: The European Kurtz, who has a European fiancée waiting for him back home, has a relationship with an African woman, his African mistress, as the author writes. The exotic could also justify the desire of back Caribbean men (in Martinique, for instance) to go to bed with white sex workers in Europe, as the famous theorist and psychoanalyst Frantz Fanon from Martinique puts it in his seminal oeuvre, *Black Skin White Masks* (1952).

A new turning point towards the process of depigmentation is at the center of a social or popular movement in Burkina Faso, a country which is so much read about in the news these days, since a seized power in 2022. Several decisions, some of which are often seen as drastic or radical but cherished by Pan-African leftist militants, scholars, or citizens. A popular association re-emerged and stressed the necessity of "condemning" skin bleaching because of its nuisance to citizens' health. In countries that share a border with

Burkina Faso, skin bleaching is embraced by all sexes; both men and women adore lightening their skin and then go an extra mile in order to achieve their goal. This fight against skin whitening is not a nascent thing in Burkina. In February 2022, the same association, the African Association to Stop Depigmentation (IASD in French), called African women to value their skin and "get rid of all complexes". The association is said to be apolitical, non-profit, and secular. In 2022, research showed that 50% of Burkinabè women used skin-lightening products. The president of the IASD lamented the fact that "coming across a waxed black complexion is becoming increasingly rare among women". He added that women go through the process because they perceive light skin as seductive, and a considerable proportion of men encourage their wives in the practice. These statements were made during a press briefing; the leaders of the IASD made strong statements in favor of black skin and refuted the inferiority complex that leads to skin whitening.

It is striking to find out that barely two years later, the same debate and crusade resurfaced, spearheaded by the same body, IASD. They probably thought that the time was ripe to have their agenda approved by the Burkinabè population and the revolutionary regime in power. The difference is that this time, the IASD meticulously pointed out through the media what they consider the roots of this failure and the devastating drawbacks it carries. They recalled the colonial origin of skin bleaching and the inferiority complex that was inculcated in blacks during that period. While I find the aim of IASD to be noble and worth defending, I am tempted to think that research should be done on the origins of the practice. Although it is sustained by an inferiority complex, skin bleaching could be older than the colonial days. On the other hand, one could "bail the association out" with the argument that they traced depigmentation to colonization in order to make their stance and message clear to populations. The dangers associated with the practice (most of them are health-related and social in nature) were listed in clear terms for the education of the masses: skin diseases, respiratory complications, cancer, and jeopardizing the life of babies in the case of pregnant women. That could sell the policy and ideals of the association, since healthcare is one of the priorities of the current Burkinabè government.

Other repulsive consequences of the practice were disclosed, and some of them were said to be more acute when the depigmentation process goes wrong. The following were listed: living with a complexion that is neither dark nor light, a process whose victims are called "taxi" in Burkinabè parlance and they are ridiculed. The vulnerability of the youth, especially females, was cited, and the speakers added that the desire to look lighter, prettier, and more beautiful leads young ladies into that, at times, under the nose of their parents, who would not say anything. The enormous negative consequences were reiterated by a lady who used to indulge in the practice. The control of the importation of products into the country is said to be one of the strategies that could alleviate the problem. Many kinds of mixture of pomade, oil, soap, and a combination whose effect on human health is negative are the products used in most cases. The financial cost of the practice is said to reach approximately 50,000 CFA (100 USD), the highest price, and is disbursed by a large number of women in a country that is battling against basic underdevelopment discomforts. The organization wrote a letter to the transitional president and requested a tightening of certain rules and regulations, a decision that could dissuade the use of skin-lightening products.

This initiative could provide several benefits for African populations and all those who patronize skin bleaching. Those positive changes could be material, economic, social, and a positive mental predisposition. The message of IASD should be heeded on all continents.

FRANCE VENTS HER ANGER ON BLACK JOURNALISTS

The debacle of France in Africa is no longer news. In the former French colonies of Africa, Paris has been booted out. That anti-French sentiment took a very obvious form in African Francophone countries that experienced coups between 2021 and 2023. While some were genuine manifestations of the anger of the African masses against the neocolonialist policy and politics of France, others were less trenchant politically and looked like palace coups orchestrated by France. Burkina Faso, Mali, and Niger belong to the first category of coups d'état I referred to; Gabon and Chad (the case of Chad is slightly more nuanced) are affiliated with the French machinations. The coup in Guinea is also a veiled color, since no clear break from Françafrique is being heard from Conakry.

The African youth is fed up with Françafrique and its tentacles. In other words, the postcolonial influence, domination, and exploitation of African countries by France has reached the epoch of its end. When Côte d'Ivoire, Gabon, Zaire (today's DRC) were led respectively by Houphouet-Boigny, Omar Bongo and his "heir", Ali Bongo, Mobutu Sese Seko, France had a tight grip on these countries, that were strategically chosen as zones of occupation and terrains of watch towers, lands whose leaders were at the beck and call of France, points from which military operations could be launched to defend French interests in Africa. Of course, the influence of France still prevails in some of those countries, unfortunately: Alassane Ouattara in Côte d'Ivoire, Mahamat Déby in Chad, and General Brice Oligui Nguema in Gabon cannot be cited when the demise of Françafrique is uttered. These leaders are clinging in one way or another to the ties of the "support" that France provides.

General Nguema, who deposed Ali Bongo in a coup, paid special visits to Alassane Ouatarra and Emmanuel Macron. French military bases remain in N'Djamena and other areas in Chad. While this continuation of the French neocolonialism in the postcolony is true in those countries, in Burkina Faso, Mali, and Niger, the general population kicked the French out. The US paid a little bit in this policy of "delinking" from neocolonialism, imperialism, and exploitation. In Niger, for instance, both the French and American politico-military apparati were dismissed. That general rebellion against France in her backyard in Africa is one of the most painful blows that could be administered to Paris. The ebullition of anti-French sentiments led several political leaders and commentators to speculate. Some French political analysts who are more enlightened and capable of objective and clairvoyant judgment simply say that the era of the French manipulation of Africa has come to an end. On the other hand, some conservative and hardcore defenders of French hegemony in Africa play ostrich by turning a blind eye to the maturity of the conscience of the African populations, especially the youth, in this era of social media. French President Macron, who has the misfortune to be steering the affairs of the Elysée during that period of politico-economic defeat of France, keeps acting like the "teacher" in French-speaking Africa.

Other French dignitaries like Anne Sophie Avé, the ambassador of France to Africa (the whole continent), unveil their myopic views of the French rejection in Africa. To make matters worse, that French "super ambassador" accuses two prominent black chroniclers living in France of instigating the rejection of France in Africa. These two black political analysts are Alain FOKA, a native of Cameroon, and Claudy SIAR, who hails originally from Guadeloupe in the Caribbean. It does not come as a surprise when the ambassador frames these media persons as the makers of anti-French positions in Africa. Each of them is an energetic, intelligent, and profound analyst and critic of the African facet of geopolitics. FOKA studied political Science, journalism, and audiovisual Arts in France, then worked with Radio France International (RFI) for 25 years before he resigned and decided to devote his time and talents to the observation, analysis, and reportage of social, political, and economic occurrences in Africa. He produced a large number of documentaries on African leaders like Thomas Sankara of Burkina Faso, interviewed the current Burkinabè President Captain Traoré, aired a program on the resources of DRC, and much more. One of the most gigantic achievements of Mr. FOKA is his creation of the Manssah project, which he manages with other partners. Manssah and its work speak to the radical Pan-Africanist position of Alain FOKA. The main goal of that information program is to "rethink Africa".

The second innocent victim of the French is Claudy SIAR, a 51-year-old journalist who has been working for Radio France International for 26 years, the same French media house where FOKA worked. Claudy SIAR was vehemently propagating and defending Afro-Caribbean culture. His main medium is a music program on the same Radio France; he openly asserts his Pan-African devotion and defends the rights of Blacks in France. He is popularly known to be "someone who is defined by Africa, not a mere lover of Africa". SIAR said several times that his native Guadeloupe is "full of Africanity, Caribbeanity and Europeanity, but the foundation of these cultures and values is the Africanity". It is said that several voices (certainly from conservative France) are calling for the dismissal of Mr. SIAR from the mega French media house, because of his blatant defense of Pan-Africanism and opposition to racism and French imperialism in Africa and the Caribbean. These two black men of culture define the current changes in Africa as "the manifestation of the pro-African ideology, mentality and sentiment that emerged in the African youth, as a result of geopolitical events on the continent", especially the skirmishes and woeful pillage by France. So, to certain French spokespersons like the ambassador to Africa, Mrs. Anne Sophie Avé, France lost its influence in Africa because of the pro-African and Pan-Africanist coverage and analyses of Alain FOKA and Claudy SIAR. She does not trace this defeat and rejection to any other source, apart from the tedious work of the two men.

Alain FOKA answered the super ambassador of France in a befitting way by pointing out the shallowness of her statement and stance that equates Pro-African and Pan-Africanism with anti-French. While Claudy SIAR did not react openly, he still goes on, unperturbed, with his powerful, efficient, radical, and objective observation of the geopolitical scene, especially its black dimension that transpires through culture; to SIAR, Pan-Africanism is Humanism. It is such a pity to see so-called first-class political figures of France venting their frustration on two innocent media persons and discerning activists.

It is more disheartening to hear a high-class French ambassador committing the mistake of seeing Pro-Africa as anti-French. What could be the way out for France is a sincere and truthful evaluation of their relations with Africa in order to find out what can provide the French with the riches that they looted in Africa for more than a century.

FIRST BLACK MAN TO WIN THE MOST PRESTIGIOUS PRIZE IN ARCHITECTURE

The Pritzker Prize is the most prestigious prize in Architecture, like what the Nobel Prize is in other areas. March 15, 2022, will remain a lodestar in History; the Pritzker Prize was awarded to a black man for the first time, and to add more to the breakthrough, the winner is an African: Burkinabè Diébédo Francis KÉRÉ.

Humble Beginnings

56-year-old KÉRÉ hails from Gando, a village located 200 kilometers from Ouagadougou in Burkina Faso, in the Centre East Region, with a population of approximately 3,000 inhabitants. Born and raised in an area where very few children have access to Western education; with no potable water and almost non -existent health care facilities, KÉRÉ was sent to school (the first child in his community to have done so) because his father wanted his son to be able to write and read letters for him, one day. The laureate refers to his background in the following terms and one finds here his early love for communalistic life, sense of space and how space configuration and comfort are related: "I grew up in a community where there was no kindergarten, but where community was your family, I remember the room where my grandmother would sit and tell stories with a little light, while we would huddle close to each other and her voice inside the room enclosed us, summoning us to come closer and form a safe place. This was my first sense of architecture". At the age of seven, he found himself crammed into an extremely hot classroom with more than 100 other students. He then started dreaming of building cooler structures later in life. This experience of poor building facilities at school in his community was his earliest inspiration to improve the educational lives of Burkina Faso's children, using architecture.

At an early age, he was sent to a neighboring town to learn traditional building techniques. Later, through a scholarship, he moved to Germany and started studying architecture at the Technical University of Berlin in 1995. KÉRÉ ultimately became an architect who combines traditional architecture with the modern one, that of his hometown with the Western ones. He is a brilliant example of an African who trained in the West and succeeds in harmoniously putting his "heterogeneous" expertise to use by helping his native community in Burkina as well as other parts of the world. He is a trained engineer who combines traditional building materials with modern engineering methods.

KÉRÉ's Style and Oeuvre

As someone who has a holistic view of Art, this architect is not moved by construction only; he rubs shoulders with other artists whose works he admires, and that certainly contributes to his distinct style. His collaboration with the German theater director Christoph Schlingensief led to the construction of a multidisciplinary arts, education, and health center in Burkina Faso, known as the Opera Village Africa (Operndorf Afrika), an arts education project located in Ouagadougou but with strong ramifications in Germany. Based in Berlin, Francis Kéré founded the Kéré Foundation in order to fund the construction of a primary school in his hometown of Gando. He links architecture to space, cities, education, and the future, an extraordinary vision that many lack in Africa. His foresightedness and ingenuity of thought transpires in statements like the following: "Architecture is an instrument we can use to create better cities, to create space to inspire people, to create classrooms which inspire the best generation" In 1998, Francis Kéré launched a project to build a school in his native village, convinced of the fact that education was the first step for the personal and economic development of his community. Three rectangular modules connected by a single roof make up the basic structure of the building, and each one of them accommodates one classroom for fifty students. The ceiling and walls are built with clay bricks, made on site by the villagers themselves. To ensure natural ventilation and protect the school from rain and sunlight, the ceramic ceiling and zinc roof are separated by a light steel lattice. The Primary School received the Aga Khan Award for Architecture in 2004 (a prize that rewards building projects that address the needs of societies with a large Muslim population), and more importantly, it became a landmark of community pride. As the collective knowledge of construction began to spread and inspire Gando, new cultural and educational projects have since been introduced for further support to sustainable development in the village. One of the techniques that only KÉRÉ masters is a construction style that creates appropriate ventilation, temperature, and light in the same structure because of the materials used, the angles, and shapes of windows and other openings. The Pritzker Prize facilitators noted that in their announcement: "A poetic expression of light is consistent throughout Kéré's works. Rays of sun filter into buildings, courtyards, and intermediary spaces, overcoming harsh midday conditions to offer places of serenity or gathering."

Internationally Acclaimed Buildings

Many of KERE's chef's d'oeuvre has attracted immense admiration. Beyond his designs in Burkina Faso, the award-winning architect has also designed permanent and temporary structures across Europe and the United States, such as London's 2017 Serpentine Pavilion. Each year, the Serpentine Gallery invites an international architect to build their first-ever London edifice on its grounds. His inspiration for the design was the trees in his home village of Gando, with structures that sought to connect the visitors with the surrounding nature. Mr. Kéré has also done designs for the famous Coachella Valley Music and Arts Festival, which runs each year in California and attracts celebrities and big names in the entertainment industry with Billie Eilish, Swedish House Mafia and Kanye West among those set to perform this year. Mr. Kéré's design for the 2019 festival was named Sarbalé Ke, which means House of Celebration in his mother tongue. His inspiration for the structure was the Baobab tree, a transposition into the West of the African traditional way and habit of peaceful meetings, fruitful discussions and amicable settlement of disputes. The laureate was very emotional and did not expect such a distinction. He claims he was simply engrossed in bringing positive transformation into his community, in Burkina, in Germany and "putting his signature" to other parts of the world. The Burkinabè

Diébédo Francis KÉRÉ's work earns blacks all over the world a special accolade, distinction and achievement.

Mmap Nonfiction and Academic books

If you have enjoyed *Pulse of the Sub-Saharan Dunes* consider these other fine **Mmap Nonfiction and Academic books** from *Mwanaka Media and Publishing:*

Cultural Hybridity and Fixity by Andrew Nyongesa
Tintinnabulation of Literary Theory by Andrew Nyongesa
South Africa and United Nations Peacekeeping Offensive Operations by Antonio Garcia
A Case of Love and Hate by Chenjerai Mhondera
A Cat and Mouse Affair by Bruno Shora
The Scholarship Girl by Abigail George
The Gods Sleep Through It All by Wonder Guchu
PHENOMENOLOGY OF DECOLONIZING THE UNIVERSITY: Essays in the Contemporary Thoughts of Afrikology by Zvikomborero Kapuya
Africanization and Americanization Anthology Volume 1, Searching for Interracial, Interstitial, Intersectional and Interstates Meeting Spaces, Africa Vs North America by Tendai R Mwanaka
Africa, UK and Ireland: Writing Politics and Knowledge Production Vol 1 by Tendai R Mwanaka
Writing Language, Culture and Development, Africa Vs Asia Vol 1 by Tendai R Mwanaka, Wanjohi wa Makokha and Upal Deb
Zimbolicious: An Anthology of Zimbabwean Literature and Arts, Vol 3 by Tendai Mwanaka
Drawing Without Licence by Tendai R Mwanaka
Writing Grandmothers/ Escribiendo sobre nuestras raíces: Africa Vs Latin America Vol 2 by Tendai R Mwanaka and Felix Rodriguez
Nationalism: (Mis)Understanding Donald Trump's Capitalism, Racism, Global Politics, International Trade and Media Wars, Africa Vs North America Vol 2 by Tendai R Mwanaka
It Is Not About Me: Diaries 2010-2011 by Tendai Rinos Mwanaka

Chitungwiza Mushamukuru: An Anthology from Zimbabwe's Biggest Ghetto Town by Tendai Rinos Mwanaka

The Day and the Dweller: A Study of the Emerald Tablets by Jonathan Thompson

Zimbolicious Anthology Vol 4: An Anthology of Zimbabwean Literature and Arts by Tendai Rinos Mwanaka and Jabulani Mzinyathi

Parks and Recreation by Abigail George

FAMILY LAW AND POLITICS WITH BIOLOGY AND ROYALTY IN AFRICA AND NORTH AMERICA by Peter Ateh-Afec Fossungu

Writing Robotics, Africa Vs Asia, Vol 2 by Tendai Rinos Mwanaka

Zimbolicious Anthology Vol 5: An Anthology of Zimbabwean Literature and Arts by Tendai R. Mwanaka

Love Notes: Everything is Love, An Anthology of Indigenous Languages of Africa and East Europe by Tendai R Mwanaka

Zimbolicious Anthology Vol 6: An Anthology of Zimbabwean Literature and Arts by Tendai R. Mwanaka and Chenjerai Mhondera

BATTLING LANGUAGE RIGHTS GOVERNANCE IN AFRICA: SWISSELGIANISM, UBACKISM, AND THE AMBAZONIA-CAMEROUN WAR by Peter Ateh-Afec Fossungu

Otherness and Pathology: The Fragmented Self and Madness in Contemporary African Fiction by Andrew Nyongesa

Zimbabwe: The Urgency of Now by Tendai Rinos Mwanaka

Zimbabwe: The Blame Game, Recollected essays and Non-fictions by Tendai Rinos Mwanaka

The Trick is to Keep Breathing: Covid 19 Stories From African and North American Writers, Vol 3 by Tendai Rinos Mwanaka

Recentring Mother Earth by Andrew Nyongesa

Zimbabwe: Beyond Robert Mugabe by Tendai Rinos Mwanaka

Language, Thought, Art and Existence: New and Recollected Essays and Non Fictions by Tendai Rinos Mwanaka

Experimental Writing, Africa Vs Latin America Vol 1 by Tendai Rinos Mwanaka and Ricardo Felix Rodriguez

HISTORY IN HISTORY OF AMBAZONIA RESISTENCE by Peter Afec-Ateh Fossungu
Zimbolicious 10th Anniversary Anthology: New and Collected Non-fictions by Tendai Rinos Mwanaka
Letters to Dariah by Rumbi Chen
THE KALEIDOSCOPE OF LIFE: Essays on Identity and Indigenous Knowledge Systems by Sithembe Isaac Xhegwana

Upcoming books

https://facebook.com/MwanakaMediaAndPublishing